WORDS THAT WORK

WORDS THAT WORK

How to Get Kids to Do Almost Anything

Alicia Eaton

The information contained in this book is intended to be educational
and not for diagnosis, prescription or treatment of any kind of health disorder
whatsoever. This information should not replace consultation with a competent
health care professional. The content of this book is intended to be used
as an adjunct to a rational and responsible health care programme prescribed
by a health care practitioner. The author and publisher are in no way liable
for any misuse of the material.

Matador
9 Priory Business Park,
Wistow Road, Kibworth Beauchamp,
Leicestershire. LE8 0RX
Tel: (+44) 116 279 2299
Fax: (+44) 116 279 2277
Email: books@troubador.co.uk
Web: www.troubador.co.uk/matador

ISBN 978 1784623 715

British Library Cataloguing in Publication Data.
A catalogue record for this book is available from the British Library.

Printed and bound in the UK by TJ International, Padstow, Cornwall
Typeset in 11pt Palatino by Troubador Publishing Ltd, Leicester, UK

Matador is an imprint of Troubador Publishing Ltd

To my daughter Clementine – currently working as one of the 'tough young teachers in the East End of London' on the Teach First scheme.

Clem - may the information in this book help you through the many challenges you face each and every day.

And to George and Tom – thank you all for making our time at The Brambles so special.

ACKNOWLEDGEMENTS

My gratitude goes to the many awesome teachers who have informed my work over the years, in particular Paul McKenna and also Richard Bandler (the co-creator of NLP). This book would not exist without them. A huge thank you also to Teena Lyons, Orla Palmer, Elaine Ridout and Maggie Langley – each of you has helped me in your own way. And to my dear friend, colleague and mentor Michele Paradise, for her ongoing love and support.

Contents

SECTION 1 – GETTING STARTED   1

Introduction   3
Chapter 1:   Honey, I Hypnotised the Kids   9
Chapter 2:   Words that Work – Your Dictionary   19

SECTION 2 – WORDS IN ACTION   57

Chapter 3:   Day-to-Day Tantrums, Rows & Flare-ups   59
Chapter 4:   Eliminating Fears and Anxiety   84
Chapter 5:   Boosting Confidence   101
Chapter 6:   Changing Unwanted Habits and Behaviours   116
Chapter 7:   Homework and Exam Stress   128
Chapter 8:   Fussy Eating and Mealtime Challenges   146
Chapter 9:   Junk Food Cravings and Weight Issues   159
Chapter 10:   Sleep and Bedtime Problems   174

SECTION 3 – PUTTING IT INTO PRACTICE   187

Chapter 11:   Your Parenting Toolkit   189
              – What exactly is your problem?   189
              – Family Conference or Meeting   197
              – Praise and Rewards   208
              – The 80/20 Rule   214
              – Turning Your Wishes into Goals   219
Chapter 12:   Get Into The Right State   224

A Final Note   242
Your 21-Day Success Journal   245

SECTION ONE

GETTING STARTED

Introduction

Wouldn't it be fantastic if you could simply wave a magic wand at kids to get them to do as you'd asked, first time around?

There's nothing more exhausting than chasing after children and constantly repeating yourself, is there? Too many parents – and teachers for that matter – struggle to get their requests **heard,** **understood** and **taken seriously** as kids just don't seem to be able to do as they're told nowadays.

Well, stop for a moment and just imagine a life where you could have much more control over:

- Embarrassing supermarket tantrums
- Sibling fights that drive you mad
- Arguments about mobile phones and screen time
- Homework routines and exam stress
- Fussy-eating and mealtime squabbles

Sounds too good to be true?

Well, it's easier to achieve than you think. You see, parents who seem to just 'get it right' and have well-behaved, high-achieving kids are not simply 'lucky'. They're doing things differently and anything they've got – you can have too.

I can't quite give you a magic wand, but I can certainly show you how to put the 'magic' back into your parenting.

But first, let me tell you a little bit about myself and my journey into 'Magic Parenting', as I like to call it.

I wasn't the perfect mother by any stretch of the imagination, but I did love being with children and made them my priority. So much so, that when my children were born I trained to be a Montessori Teacher. When I opened my own School, my two year-old daughter became my very first pupil.

But life doesn't always run smoothly and a few years later it threw me a curve ball. My ex-husband and I separated and I was propelled into life as a single parent with three of the most boisterous, energetic and exhausting kids imaginable.

Simple things like shopping became a nightmare. There was no online shopping in those days and being a single mum meant the children had to go absolutely everywhere with me. I had no-one to leave them with at home and no grandparents or relatives close-by to help out.

Like most parents, I resorted to shouting and yelling at my children. How else could I stop them from swinging on the sitting room curtains, tearing them down with their Tarzan impersonations?

It wasn't long before life began to feel like a tight elastic band that was about to go snap. In those days, 'success' meant nothing more than getting through the week in order to start it all again on Monday morning. Life was miserable and exhausting.

Things came to a head one particularly bad weekend. The arguments started the moment I picked the kids up from school on Friday afternoon and thereafter, everything we did and said to each other seemed to clash and jar. Each exchange of words escalated to new levels of anger and frustration.

It was a dreadful weekend and if we weren't all shouting and arguing, then we were barely speaking to each other. It was horrible. I hated it and the children hated it. I remember it to be one of the loneliest weekends I'd ever experienced. Whilst I was sharing a house with three other individuals, our only form of communication was to scowl at each other – I felt utterly isolated and alone.

Something was triggered inside me that weekend. I realised that as a single parent, if I didn't get along with my children, then I wasn't going to have anyone to talk to. No-one to tell my news to. No-one to have fun with on holidays and weekends. I started to wonder if ever again I'd arrive home and be greeted by someone who would ask me how I was or if I'd had a good day? Was this how life was going to be for the next ten or so years?

I knew things had to change. I lived with three fantastic, interesting, lively, fun-loving human beings. So, there really was no need to be lonely at all – it was simply a question of learning to how to live with each other and enjoy each other's company.

I reflected back on the mood and atmosphere that I'd cultivated in my Montessori classroom. Certainly, my children were older and my eldest George in particular, was a never ending whirling ball of energy, but still… I knew from experience how easy it could be to instil a sense of peace and calm in the classroom with just the sound of my voice. Getting kids to listen and follow my instructions, without shouting and yelling, was the most important part of my job.

I thought a bit more about how easy it is for us parents to fall into bad habits when speaking to children and once we have, how difficult it is to get out of the hole that we inevitably dig for ourselves. I listened in to other parents' conversations – perhaps you've done the same thing yourself, at the supermarket say? How many of us have cringed when we've heard a parent lose it with a young child when they're out shopping? It's not a pleasant experience, is it?

The last piece of the jigsaw puzzle fell into place for me when I moved on from the Montessori School and trained as a Clinical Hypnotherapist and NLP (Neuro-Linguistic Programming) Practitioner. I was fortunate to be trained by some of the top people in this field, including Paul McKenna, who I went on to assist for many years.

From this point on, my life began to change. My training taught me all about the *'Language of Persuasion'* – which words work and which ones not to bother using. I quickly learned how to slip a little 'hypnotic influence' shall we say, into general conversation and noticed how much easier asking kids to do things became.

I changed the way I spoke and sure enough, our lives changed. My children stopped bickering – we became good friends and their talents began to shine through. The following years produced some of the happiest moments for all of us and I feel lucky that we were able to feel so close to each other.

Today, I'd like to see other parents and children have the same positive experiences, so I've decided it's time to spill the beans. Politicians, TV advertisers and sales people know exactly which words persuade and influence us the most. In fact, people are 'persuading' us to do things all the time, only more often than not, we simply don't realise it.

Of course, they like to keep all of this a secret but I'm going to share their strategies with you so that you too, can have a happy family life. I'll teach you which words work and which ones don't and I'll also explain the key language patterns used by some of the most successful people in the world. I've adapted them for parents and teachers just like you, to make life in the home or the classroom so much easier.

You'll discover how changing the structure of your sentences and the words you choose, will put an end to:

- The endless nagging and yelling that wears you out, but gets you nowhere.
- Those reward systems and star charts that cost you money but quickly lose their appeal.
- The frustration caused by your children's inability to follow the simplest of requests.

Your life will become easier and in a happier, more relaxed environment, you and your children can start having the kind of relationship that perhaps you'd only been able to dream of before.

So let me tell you about this system – I've divided this book into three sections like so:

In **Section One**: I explain exactly how your child's subconscious mind randomly absorbs everything in its' path and interprets what you're saying. I think it's a good idea for you to have an understanding of the psychology behind some of the problems. And then, I tell you all about the clever words and phrases that are ideal for using with your family and which ones are best avoided. You'll have your very own Dictionary to refer to.

In **Section Two**: I'll show you how to put those words "into action" and apply them to some of the most commonly encountered problems. So whether the issue is mealtime arguments over fussy eating or junk food cravings; an anxiety or phobia about dogs, spiders, going to school or exams; a lack of confidence; bad habits such as nail-biting, thumbsucking or bedwetting, rows over screen time, homework or bedtimes, you'll quickly learn what to say and what not to say.

In **Section Three**: You can put your newfound knowledge into practice, using my unique Toolkit of Parenting. I'll show you how to take stock of your life and how to figure out what needs tackling and changing first. Here, you'll find advice on getting into the right state both mentally and physically, in order to make those vital changes that you need. There's also my unique 'Success4Kids' 21-Day step-by-step Success Journal specially designed to help you stick to your new routines. You'll be able to identify family hotspots, prioritise changes, focus on solutions and create clear goals.

The ideas featured in this book will help you to have the kind of successful and rewarding relationship with your children that I experienced, after I made these changes. Looking back, I'm so grateful that the combination of my specialist trainings enabled me to reverse the downward spiral we were on, before it was too late.

I know it's a bit of a cliché to say that children grow up quickly and one day you'll look back wistfully wondering where the time went, but I know just how true this is – one day it will all be just a memory. Whether it's a bad one or a good one, is up to you now.

We only get one chance to be a parent to our kids – so who wants to go to the trouble and expense of having them, to then see those precious moments ruined by arguments, tears and tantrums. Yours – and theirs!

Everything you do and say today is creating that memory for the future and fortunately, it's never too late to turn it into something that everyone in the family wants to remember forever.

In the next section, you'll find your all important 'Words that Work Dictionary' – prepare to be amazed at how easy it is to powerfully influence someone, just by changing one word or the structure of your sentence. You'll never trust a salesperson or believe a TV advert again!

1

Honey, I Hypnotised the Kids

"Hypnosis started when the first mother kissed it and made it better"

F. BAUMAN

When people learn that I'm a Clinical Hypnotherapist, one of the first questions they invariably ask is: 'have you ever *hypnotised* your own children?' And usually, they'll whisper it behind their hands, eyes wide in shock.

I suspect they visualise some sort of stage hypnosis act where I use a few well chosen words, delivered in a soporific tone, sending my poor, un-witting kids 'under' before I deliver my message and then bring them round with a click of my fingers.

While nothing could be further from the truth, I confess I usually avoid giving a full explanation, because I can see their minds are probably already made up. Instead, I generally give a stock reply that probably only answers half the question and don't go into too many details. But today, I'm going to come clean. I ADMIT IT! In the past, I have *hypnotised* my kids.

Now, before you jump up in horror wondering if it's illegal, or at the very least immoral, let me share something else with you.

You have *hypnotised* your kids too!

Not once, or twice, or every now and then, but each and every day!

I don't mean in the dramatic staged manner that everyone associates with the word hypnosis. You, me and every parent or teacher in the land "hypnotise" children with the words we use, all the time.

Your words are constantly being absorbed by your child's subconscious mind and have a profound effect on their thinking, their feelings and their behaviour. You may never have considered what it was you were doing or, if you have, you will have called it something entirely different, but trust me: it's hypnosis.

And guess what?

At times, your children have hypnotised you too.

Don't believe me?

Children hypnotise their parents all the time! Why else would find yourself purchasing the toys, sweets and treats that you told your child in no uncertain terms, you'd not be buying?

One minute you're standing there telling your child that there's no way they're going to get a treat at the shops today and the next minute, you find yourself going home with said treat and a child skipping with glee.

Feels strange, doesn't it? How did that happen, we ask.

And in order to feel better, we kid ourselves that it was a conscious decision to deviate from the plan, justifying it by coming up with the perfect excuse – 'OK, I'll let you have a treat this afternoon – but only this once, mind – and only because we're going out next Saturday and there won't be time to get your usual weekend treat then'. But in your mind, you already know that this won't be the case and you'll be buying a second treat at the weekend as usual.

Your child's highly persuasive powers were at work here.

We often hear parents use the term 'pester power', but interestingly each child's pestering is slightly different. They quickly learn how to push their parents' buttons by modifying and changing the words they use, till they get the result they want.

Now, at last, it's your turn – it's time to take the power back. With a little extra insight into how profoundly language can influence behaviour, you'll discover how easy it can be to do just that.

HOW DOES IT ALL WORK?

The language of persuasion and influence works in much the same way that TV adverts brainwash people into buying a certain brand of tea. Once a message has been deeply absorbed by our subconscious minds, it's pretty much stuck there – a bit like a tattoo.

It's the reason why most of us will buy the same brand of tea week-after-week throughout our life – in many cases, it's the same brand that our parents bought too. But in most cases, we're not making a conscious choice to buy that brand – it's just that it feels 'odd' to buy a different one, almost an act of betrayal. Which of course, is exactly how the manufacturers want us to feel.

But, if it's so easy to hypnotise someone into doing something – even a chimp on a TV advert can do it – how come we often feel so powerless when it comes to controlling our children's behaviour? After all, it should be simple – shouldn't it?

Well yes, it should be – but most of us seem to tie ourselves up in knots and struggle to get our message across. But, as I know only too well, with just a little bit of inside knowledge, life can become a whole lot easier.

I wonder if you were one of the many children who grew up struggling to do maths at school, simply because a teacher had told you that you'd never be any good at maths – or you'd heard that "maths is difficult" from your parents or friends. Not only did the overwhelming majority of us believe them but we went on to prove them right too. A self-fulfilling prophecy – for what we believe, we become.

If it's that easy to influence behaviour, imagine how powerful it could be if you had a better understanding of which words work and which ones most definitely don't. You could guide and 'persuade' your children to not only do the things you want them to do, without all the stress and arguments, but also develop their skills, talents and full potential.

Just think, who could you have been, if you'd been given the right encouragement at the right time?

But, before we get ourselves all fired up about our less than perfect upbringings and all those missed opportunities, let's remember that it's not possible to change the past but it is possible to influence the future.

And this is your opportunity to do things differently.

Remember, YOU are creating your child's future right now.

YOUR CHILD'S HYPNOTIC MIND

So let's take a few moments to understand exactly what is going on inside a young child's mind as they grow and develop.

If you've ever felt 'in two minds' about something, it's because two minds is exactly what you have. Your conscious mind can think about the past, present and future. It's the bit that reminds you to make that phone call or buy a loaf of bread on the way home.

The subconscious mind, far from being an old filing cabinet, is actually more like the motor or engine that drives you. Having been programmed from childhood by your environment and the experiences you've had, it stores all your habits and behaviours and acts like your personal automatic pilot. We all have one, but everyone's is slightly different.

The subconscious mind does much more than simply 'remember' the constant repetition of actions, habits, thoughts and ideas that go into it. This barrage of information actually 'creates' the subconscious mind – and so, creates you.

Most of us have driven a car, reached our destinations and worried that we couldn't remember a thing about the journey. Well, you can worry no more, for your subconscious mind did the driving for you. Remember how you programmed it with all those hours of expensive driving lessons? This conveniently leaves your conscious mind free to think about all sorts of other things. You can chat to your friends, sing-along to the radio, eat a sandwich and arrive at your destination without remembering how you got there. Slightly worrying, isn't it? Your subconscious mind operated on autopilot whilst your conscious mind was set to manual.

It's a very clever system that prevents us from having to do everything from scratch each time we do it – we simply no longer have to 'think' about it. I'm sure you've already seen this in action with your own child. Remember when they first learned how to tie their shoelaces or write their own name? Their faces were screwed up in concentration, perhaps with a tongue poking out.

After a while though, they got the hang of it and now they tie their laces or write their name without thinking about it or even needing to look at what they're doing. The behaviour pattern is imprinted on the subconscious mind.

Your child's subconscious mind is pretty much 'empty' to begin with and gradually gets programmed with all the experiences their environment gives them. It's what gives human beings the advantage over animals – we can adapt to our environment precisely because we're not fully formed at birth. If you pick up a newly born giraffe and stick him in the North Pole, he won't survive for very long for the possibility of growing a shaggy warm coat is not open to him.

Pick up a human baby, on the other hand and transfer him from the UK to Japan and within a few short years he'll quickly become fluent in Japanese with no trace of an accent whatsoever. He'll adapt.

Your child's mind is open and ready to receive everything you put in his path. In fact, it could be said that your child is in a state of 'waking hypnosis' – and you as the parent, are programming that mind with all the things that you say and do.

It's not uncommon to hear the phrase 'in one ear and out the other' when talking about children's seemingly limited listening abilities, but take it from me, even if they appear not to be listening, your words and actions are being absorbed and are not just being remembered but are actually 'creating' your child.

As adults, we can be a bit more picky and choosy about which things to think and believe. But young minds randomly absorb all sorts of ideas and beliefs that become 'true' to them. That's why it's so easy to convince kids about made up stories of Father Christmas, Tooth Fairies and Easter Bunnies.

Parents usually feel pretty embarrassed when they hear their child say their very first swear word. If they're honest though, it's not because of the word itself, but the fact that it comes out with the correct pronunciation and nuance – it has Mum or Dad's signature all over it.

THE GHOST OF CHRISTMAS PAST

This childhood imprinting can be the cause of many arguments – especially at traditional events that naturally have a stream of emotions attached, such as a family wedding or Christmas. It's not uncommon, for example, for young married couples to fall out over festive arrangements. *'What do you mean you don't want to eat turkey? I don't care if your family always ate duck on Christmas Day – we can't possibly have Christmas without a turkey!'* or *'But I'm used to opening presents as soon as everyone wakes up – what do you mean we're 'supposed' to wait till after lunch to do that?'* Seemingly trivial details become monumentally important with everyone appearing to be 'selfish' for not wanting to budge.

And the arguments get worse of course, with the arrival of children, for each parent is instantly transported back to their own childhood rituals that are by now so deeply embedded in the emotional make-up, that doing anything different means it feels odd, it feels wrong and it hurts!

So that's the bad news. But I have good news for you too!

It's precisely because your children's minds are so open and receptive that using your words wisely and correctly, can create a happy, loving family for you, with kids who respond to your requests more easily than perhaps you had ever imagined.

THE SECRETS OF STAGE HYPNOSIS

Many people are scared when they hear the word 'hypnosis', even though they can't quite put their finger on why this should be. They shy away from conversations about 'programming' children's minds and influencing their behaviour as if by doing so, it won't happen. But of course it is happening – and in so many cases, the general lack of knowledge means it gets done badly. That's why I'm passionate about helping parents, teachers and anyone else who's involved in raising a child to better understand just how much influence the words we use, really have.

Quite often people's fears are based on what they've seen on stage shows and they start to wonder if they too will end up walking in a silly way and clucking like a chicken.

That's why I've decided to spill a few beans and let you in on some of the secrets.

There are a number of components to a stage show that make it seem magical. To begin with, there is the general expectation of the audience, which influences their behaviour.

They already know that some of them will be selected to behave in an extraordinary manner and this suggestion alone is enough to trigger off the exhibitionist tendencies that some of them have, especially if fuelled by alcoholic drinks beforehand. They're hyped up and feeding off each other's excitement too.

Many suggestibility tests are done on the audience beforehand: quite simple things such as asking them to stretch their arms straight out in front, close their eyes and imagine a strong glue being applied to the palms of their hands. They'll be asked to then stick their palms together as the suggestion is given that this is ultra-strong glue and they *might* struggle to release their hands.

The people that follow this instruction and do indeed find themselves unable to separate their hands, are deemed to be highly suggestible and perfect for a stage performance. They are then chosen and seated together in a separate part of the auditorium.

It's usual then for the stage hypnotist to start his act. He asks for volunteers from this pre-selected part of the audience – those with the 'sticky hands'. Those who respond to the hypnotist and put their hands up quickly to volunteer, will be chosen. By quickly, I mean those who instantly shoot their hands up in the air. Those who hesitate are rejected. So the volunteers have in effect, overcome two obstacles.

Further tests are placed in the participants' way. The hypnotist places a row of chairs on the stage – let's say he has nine chairs. He then selects ten people from the volunteers who raised their hands quickly and invites them to come up and take a seat. Of course, they're one chair short so the participant who is the slowest to respond, will be without a chair and therefore eliminated. The hypnotist is seeking super-keen people and whittling down the group as he goes.

With nine people seated on the chairs, he asks them all to stand up and then to sit back down again. The slowest to sit down can be eliminated again. At this stage, he may even reduce the group to just four or five people. He's looking for people who carry out his instructions immediately, without giving them a second thought.

And of course, these people are keen; they've come for a night out to a stage show and feel chuffed and special at having been selected to assist the star act.

The volunteers are then asked to stand up and go through a few ridiculous exercises in front of the audience. The hypnotist will be monitoring how they respond to the audience's cheers of encouragement. Those who start to let themselves go and clearly enjoy putting on a performance will get to stay with him, the others will be sent back to their seats.

This process of elimination could take a whole hour, by which time the last participant left on stage with the hypnotist is the most compliant, along with having strong exhibitionist tendencies, adrenaline-fuelled, pumped up and ready to perform.

This person is then able to behave as ridiculously as he chooses, safe in the knowledge that he can hand over responsibility for his outrageous actions to the hypnotist. And at the end of it all, he can claim he can't remember a thing and so is blameless. *"It wasn't me – I can't remember a thing!"* he'll be telling his mates on the way home.

A truly hypnotised person would not be able to perform and dance around on stage, as the sign of a deep trance is actually complete stillness. Even when we are asleep, it's common to fidget and move around, but a deliberately induced hypnotic state is an altogether much calmer place to be.

So, you can rest assured that a 'stage show' is just that – a stage show. And, quite different from the kind of experience you'd have in a session with a qualified Clinical Hypnotherapist – and certainly very different from the kind of influence I'll be helping you to have over your children's behaviour.

What I'll be teaching you is perfectly safe, it's natural and as I said earlier, your words are already 'hypnotising' your children, just not in the way you'd always like. With a little inside knowledge, you can avoid making mistakes – just as that maths teacher, or perhaps your own parents did – and have things running a little more smoothly.

2

Words That Work

Never underestimate the power of your words on a young child's life – for what you do and say now will very probably, stay with them for a lifetime.

So, let's get started: in this chapter you'll see that I've created a sort of dictionary or lexicon, to show a range of words and phrases that persuade and influence more than others. However, before we begin, here's a brief warning: it's going to be really tempting to quickly test out some of the tricks that you'll learn in this section straightaway, but I'm going to recommend that you 'keep your powder dry' for the moment.

Language is a powerful tool but only if used correctly. The last thing you want right now is to slip-up like a novice because if you do, it might be quite a while before you can have another attempt. Kids are canny little creatures and they're highly tuned to pick-up on language patterns, which is why nursery rhymes and poems appeal so much at this age.

My advice is to read through this chapter thoroughly and take your time to think about how and when you'll start implementing some of the things you'll be learning here.

WHAT YOU SEE IS WHAT YOU GET

As we think and speak, our minds are constantly creating images or pictures. They flash through our minds really quickly, so we often don't notice them.

We also have an 'internal dialogue' which is that little voice inside our head that seems to chatter away incessantly throughout the day. Sometimes, it's our own voice that we hear, but other times, it could be the voice of someone else such as a parent, a friend, schoolteacher, work colleague or family member. And it could be a critical voice, or a friendly one.

If I mention the word 'oranges' your mouth may begin to water and perhaps you'll get a flashback to the last time you ate a delicious, juicy orange. I know some of you will even be able to 'taste' it.

"What you see is what you get" is a phrase I often use with my clients, for our bodies act upon the 'instructions' we give them. They take their cue from the images and pictures that we create inside our imaginations. It doesn't matter whether they're made 'accidentally' because they're prompted by someone or something externally, or 'deliberately' because we're thinking on purpose. It's as if we're magnetically drawn towards these images.

Let's play around with a few words and pictures now and you'll see what I mean.

Exercise

Get a piece of paper and pen – or use your mobile phone to make notes.

Now, think for a moment about each of the following, taking a few moments to pause and reflect before you make a note of the details. You can close your eyes if you'd like to.

- What did you eat for dinner last night?
  Write down your answer and think about it carefully.

- What was the very first car you ever owned?
  Write down your answer and think about it carefully.

- Where would you like to go on holiday next year?
  Write down your answer and think about it carefully.

Did you notice what happened?

I'll bet you saw a picture of that old car in your head. Perhaps you could even see yourself driving it. And the plate of food – perhaps you noticed your surroundings too. Were you in a restaurant or at home? And what about that holiday? A golden sandy beach, lapped by the azure ocean, perhaps.

The reason why it's important to become aware of these pictures and any voices or sounds that happen to come with them, is because our bodies generally take these as the command, or instruction, on what to do next.

This thinking process is what helps us to get into a swimming pool and swim a particular stroke, say, breaststroke, instead of backstroke. Our arms and legs can't think for themselves. We give them an instruction through our thoughts.

Exercise

Now, next step – how about I ask you not to think of:

- A piece of chocolate cake
  Write down your answer and think about it carefully.

I wonder now, did it have a cherry on the top, chocolate sprinkles or a blob of ice-cream with it?

But wait!

I asked you NOT to think of a piece of chocolate cake. Hmmm, I bet an awful lot of you did!

So, why did that happen?

Let me explain – it's because there are no pictures for negative words like 'don't', 'no', 'not', or 'never', so our minds can only make pictures from the remaining words. Unfortunately, these remaining words frequently encapsulate exactly what we don't want to happen.

And remember, we are magnetically drawn towards these pictures.

So, how many of us have witnessed a young child being told: *"Don't touch the vase!"* Invariably, the next thing they'll do is exactly that. They won't be able to stop themselves.

The pictures that spring into their mind will be formed from the words 'touch' and 'vase' – they have no option.

And I wonder how many parents have then muttered the words *"Is he deaf? How many times have I told him not to do that!"* or worse still, *"Is he stupid?"*

So now you know. It's none of those.

To get your child to leave the vase alone, you should have told him to do just that. *"Lets leave the vase alone."* Simple. If you want a child to do something, you need to flip your sentences around into positive terms, staying away from any negative words.

Children are constantly having to visualise themselves behaving in new ways – whether it's being able to swim backstroke, ride a bike without stabilisers, kick a football, read a more advanced book or write their names.

It's the same for us adults. Hairdressers visualise a hairstyle before starting to use the scissors to cut (we hope!). We don't start to mix the ingredients for a cake without having a picture of the end result in our minds and when we get into our cars to drive, we're visualising our destination. We do this all the time. Children are mostly better at doing it than we are too.

So tapping into this 'visualisation process' is a safe and natural way to help children deal with problems.

To extend this further, if we start thinking about what we don't want (eg. not to get cross and angry) we'll only make it harder for ourselves to feel calm and relaxed. By the very act of thinking negatively, your thoughts will be subsumed by those negative pictures.

How can you possibly feel good when the picture in your mind is one of you yelling and tearing your hair out in anger and frustration? Studies have even shown that if you're feeling chilly on a winter's day, thinking about a hot, sunny beach will warm you up. Our language and thoughts have an affect on the central nervous system too.

So that's why it's so important to ask your children to do exactly what you *do want* them to do, rather than telling them to stop doing something or what you *don't want* them to do.

1. SAY WHAT YOU DO WANT, NOT WHAT YOU DON'T WANT

If you want a child to do something, you need to couch your sentences in positive terms, staying away from any negative words. Look at the following examples. Both are essentially seeking the same result, but the first version will be more successful in that outcome every time.

Let's leave the room nice and tidy
will produce a different result to saying:
Don't leave your room in a mess

Let's see if we can speed up and be early today
is much more likely to get a child moving than:
Stop being a slowcoach or we'll be late

Let's see if we can sit at the table as quiet as mice today
is better than:
Stop making a noise and mucking around

Remember to walk calmly and slowly
is better than:
Don't run

Do remember to take your PE bag in the morning
is better than:
Don't forget...... (You'll be magnetically drawn to forgetting.)

2. AVOID WORDS THAT CREATE OBSTACLES

Next time you find yourself struggling to achieve your goals have a think about the type of words you use when you speak to yourself. It could be that the words you're using are the very words that prevent you from getting them done. Avoid these:

- I must
- I should
- I ought to
- I may
- I might
- I could
- I'll try

Have you noticed that people who say 'I must', or 'I really should', often don't?

If you say to yourself; *"I must sort out the cupboards"* it will not only give you a heavy, negative feeling, but will also be creating a picture in your mind that suggests an uphill struggle. Perhaps you'll even get a picture of messy cupboards in your mind.

Whereas, if you put it differently, saying something like: *"I'm going to sort out the cupboards on Tuesday"* it puts a completely different complexion on the matter. Those words are more likely to produce a picture of clean and tidy cupboards in your mind.

Similarly, *"I ought to walk the dog"* implies that it's something that you've been putting off doing. The picture that springs to mind here might be one of an unwalked dog looking forlorn.

Think instead of the sentence; *"I will walk the dog this morning"*. This immediately creates a momentum and might conjure up an image of you and your dog striding along in the fresh air.

Notice too that I added a couple of extra words second time around; 'on Tuesday' and 'this morning'. Being more specific about your commitment and the timescales around it means you are more likely to do it.

Remember, human beings are driven by the images created in their minds. Your body will always be driven to doing what it sees itself doing in your imagination. Positive pictures create positive results and negative ones are more likely to hold you back.

The same goes with our children. Telling your child that they 'must' do their homework will only foster a bad feeling. It's far better to say; *"how about doing your spelling homework at 6.30 so that we have plenty of time for bath and bubbles at 7 o'clock?"*

Similarly, *"You should stop leaving your shoes by the front door"* would be better, and more effective if it is phrased simply as: *"Let's put all the shoes in the cupboard under the stairs"*.

3. NEVER 'TRY' ANYTHING

Follow this exercise to see how one tiny little word can so easily create a negative picture and hold you back. Why not test it out on a friend or colleague? Ask them to close their eyes and follow your instructions and have them do the same to you.

1. Close your eyes and see in your imagination a door.
2. Notice the colour of the door and say the colour out loud.
3. Open the door.
4. When you have opened the door, open your eyes.

PAUSE

5. Close your eyes again and see in your imagination another door.
6. Notice the colour of the door and say the colour out loud.
7. Now this time, try to open the door.
8. Open your eyes and come back into the room

- What difference did you find between the first door and the second door?
- Were the doors the same colour, or different?
- Did they have handles, locks or bolts?
- Were the handles on the same side?
- Did the doors open slowly or quickly?

As you'll discover, when you use the word 'try' you will either find it difficult, or you will not be able to do it at all. It's quite incredible how such a small word can have such a big impact, but it does. By automatically suggesting that whatever it is you're planning to do is going to be a struggle, it becomes just that.

This is an interesting exercise and will probably make you think back to your own childhood. How many times did someone say to you; *"as long as you try, that's all that matters"*, or *"try your best"*, or *"just try and have a go"*, or best of all *"try your hardest!"* Twice in one sentence, it has been suggested to you that you're going to struggle.

How different would the results have been if you had been given positive directions rather than those negative ones that held you back? 'Try' is definitely a word to avoid using with your kids!

4. SWITCH *ALWAYS* AND *NEVER* FOR SOMETIMES

It's interesting how easy it is to get locked into the idea of failure. Once an idea is firmly established in the mind (eg. my child is a fussy-eater), we unconsciously seek out evidence to support this idea. In other words, it becomes so automatic to remember all the times that food was refused, that we cancel out remembering any moments of success.

- *Mealtimes are always a struggle.*
- *My children never eat vegetables.*
- *My children always moan when I cook something new.*
- *Whenever I cook anything new my kids never eat it.*

Yet, change those 'always / never' words into 'sometimes' and notice how it changes your feelings.

- *Mealtimes are sometimes a struggle.*
- *My children sometimes eat vegetables.*
- *My children sometimes moan when I cook something new.*
- *Whenever I cook a new dish my kids sometimes eat it.*

Take a few moments to remember back to those moments, when your children did eat calmly or try new foods. Was it at someone else's house? At a party? On holiday? Think back to a time when their behaviour actually surprised you.

Start using the 'sometimes' on a regular basis from now on.

5. MOVE FROM *CAN'T* TO *POSSIBILITY*

The word CAN'T is used far too often in our conversations and doing so shuts out the possibility of achievement. To get out of this habit, highlight that things can and do change. Indeed, your child is changing all the time, which means not being able to do something is merely transient.
When your child says: *"I can't do maths!"*

Turn it around into: *"Ah, you just haven't yet found a way to………"*

Switch focus to talk about what your child CAN do rather than what they CAN'T:

"You can add, subtract, multiply and divide…… You just haven't yet found a way to do fractions. Don't forget, things change. We change all the time – and learning how to do fractions is just one more of those things that will gradually change."

This will shift your child's attitude.

It may help to remind your child of struggles that they've had in the past, that they then mastered:

"You know, once upon a time, you couldn't swim backstroke – do you remember? You splashed and struggled – and to be honest, even I was starting to wonder if you'd ever get the hang of it. (Add a smile and a wink to show you are teasing.) *And then, look what happened.*

All of a sudden, one day, something just clicked and now… well, now…… you're one of the best backstroke swimmers in the class."

6. *AND* IS BETTER THAN *BUT*

Picture the scene. You've got a great idea and can hardly wait to share it with the family. Perhaps it's a suggestion of where you might go on holiday this year, a film you might go to see together that weekend or what to eat for supper that night. Then, you've barely got the sentence out, describing your thought when someone pipes up with a 'but'.

"But we went to Greece last year."

Or

"But I don't like action movies."

Or

"But I don't like lasagne."

The instant rejection wrapped up in that small, three-letter word is just so demoralizing. Our children feel that same sense of dejection, so it's best to avoid using the word wherever possible and replace it with 'and'.

Thus, rather than:

Child: *"I want a biscuit."*
Adult: *"You may want a biscuit, BUT it's too close to supper time."*

Replace with:

Adult: *"Ah – you want a biscuit – AND when we've had supper, you can choose which biscuits you'd like to eat."*

Or:

Child: *"I don't like carrots!"*

Adult: *"I know you don't like them BUT they're good for you."*

Versus:

Adult: *"I know that you're not keen on eating boiled carrots AND that's why we're having raw, grated carrots today. Would like to help me? I can show you how to hold the grater."*

In both cases, the first scenario is bound to kick off an argument and debate, whereas the second will divert attention from the 'here and now'.

7. *BUT* REVERSAL

Another technique to eliminate the negative connotations around the word 'but' is to reverse the sentence surrounding it. Imagine, for example, you were in two minds about something. On the one hand you really want to do 'A', but on the other hand, you also want 'B' and that causes a conflict. You're torn.

The two sides of this dilemma are divided by the word "BUT" in the middle of the sentence. Now, notice how you can completely change the emphasis and – more importantly – your motivation by simply reversing each side:

"I really want to lose weight ... BUT ... I simply adore eating chocolate."
Becomes: *"I simply adore eating chocolate ... BUT ...I really want to lose weight."*

"I'd like to get fit ... BUT ... I hate going to the gym."
Becomes: *"I hate going to the gym ... BUT ... I'd like to get fit."*

"I'd really like to sort out my paperwork ... BUT ... I just hate filing."
Becomes: *"I hate filing ... BUT ... I'd really like to sort out my paperwork."*

The picture in your head and therefore your desire, changes completely with this simple trick of reversing your statement.

Now imagine how doing this with your child's sentences could boost their motivation for doing things that are less appealing:

"I know I've got homework to do … BUT … I want to go out and play with my friends."
Becomes:
"So, you want to go out and play … BUT … you know you've got your homework to do."

Or, in conversation:

Adult: *"It's time to turn off the TV and do your homework."*
Child: *"Oh, BUT I don't want to miss my favourite programme!"*
Adult: *"So, you don't want to miss your favourite programme – BUT you've also got your English homework to do. Which chapter do you have to read tonight? Is it the one where the King invades the other country? I can record the programme for you while you take a look at that."*

8. *BUT* CAN BE USEFUL

There are times when the word 'but' can be very useful indeed. The word can be a great tool to acknowledge other people's objections and negative feelings and then push them away from the awareness. The 'but' acts as an indication that things are going to change.

In context, it might work something like this:

"I know that as a family we haven't always got on as well as we could have… BUT…that's in the past now and we can do things differently from now on."

or

"I appreciate your concerns and reservations about whether this will work or not … BUT … I'd like you to think about this idea and let me know your thoughts tomorrow."

Or

"I know you're concerned about going back to school for the new term ... BUT ... we'll be meeting some of the new girls in your class tomorrow afternoon and that will be helpful."

9. BECOME

A very useful word is 'become'. It suggests progression, a change of direction and that things are moving forward:

"And as you become more and more relaxed about this each and every day..."

"As each week passes, you're becoming a much better swimmer..."

More words that suggest things are changing and moving forward are:

"And as you <u>start noticing</u> yourself <u>becoming</u> more and more successful with each and every attempt to......"

"As you <u>start to change</u> the way you organize your bedroom, you'll <u>quickly</u> see the difference it makes."

"<u>I can see by looking</u> at that relaxed smile on your face that a transformation <u>is taking place</u>."

"<u>You'll be surprised</u> by how quickly you'll <u>be able to stop</u> making those mistakes <u>and start</u> getting more and more of the answers right."

"That's great – <u>you've already</u> come up with three new ways of getting that done. <u>I expect</u> you've thought of a few more too."

10. *STOP*

'Stop' is another great little word to keep as part of your armoury. Using the word 'stop', followed by a command, is a very useful way of closing down resistance and argument, in order to create an opening for something new.

It is a great word to help your child pause for a moment now and just imagine that they can do something more easily. By gaining that valuable breathing space, you can encourage them to think what the alternative might look like. What would the child need to do to make things better?

Thus:

"OK, let's STOP and... picture what it could be like..."

or

"How about we STOP and think about what we will need to do to make it all right."

In Chapter Three, which focuses on tantrums and arguments, I show you how to help your child visualise a 'Stop Button' inside their mind. Each time you use the word 'Stop', the image will appear and they'll be able to stop whatever it is they're doing more easily.

11. TELL YOU

We don't usually say that we're going to 'say something' before we actually say it, so it adds a sense of importance to whatever comes next.

"I've got something important to tell you..."

"I'm going to share something with you..."

"Listen, I'm going to explain something to you..."

"I'm going to tell you something that I think you want to know......"

12. THINK ABOUT IT

Front loading a sentence with this phrase, sends a powerful suggestion that your child will indeed 'think about it'.

"Think about it. How good will it feel once you've finished your homework?"

"Think about it. Won't it be great to go to school knowing you're up to date with work?"

"Think about it. Isn't it better to look at this differently?"

13. LISTEN

The word 'listen' can have a powerful effect. Like 'think about it' it implies that whatever's being said next is important.

"OK, listen. Here's what I think needs to be done next."

"Listen... we need to quickly get our coats on or we'll miss the bus."

14. WHEN

The word 'WHEN' is often referred to as the most hypnotic word in the English language. It's what we call an implied causative – it implies a first cause.

"When you've learnt how to do backstroke, the Swimming Teacher will ask you to join the Relay Team."

This suggests that the child will indeed learn backstroke.

Or

"When you've finished your maths homework, we'll be able to go out to the park. " This suggests that the homework will be completed.

As you get better at this technique, you might even be able to fit in two presuppositions:

"When you've finished your homework, you'll notice how easy it is to solve similar problems."

Two presuppositions there: you will finish and you will find it easy.

Car salespeople often use this pattern: *"When we've been out for a test drive, we'll come back and you can choose a colour scheme for the interior."* You may not have even been asked whether you would like to take a test drive. He's pushing you along the sales process.

Other useful words that link very nicely to a presupposition are:

After you've tidied your room. (You will tidy your room)

As you do this. (You will do this)

Before you change your clothes. (Clothes will be changed)

Next time you ... (There will be a next time)

While you're thinking about your next option. (There is a next option)

Since you started making those changes. (Changes have been made)

15. CREATE THE ILLUSION OF CHOICE

Another great use of presuppositions is to create the illusion of choice. Your child will see you offering one alternative and another, but won't realise you have cleverly slipped in the fact that you pre-suppose they will do something. By using this technique, they will tacitly accept the assumption and instead focus on the 'main event' which is the choice they have been offered.

Examples of this technique would include

"Do you want to work on your school project today or tomorrow?"

Or

"Would you like to organise your school bag before or after supper?"

or

"Do you want to wear the blue t-shirt or the one with the picture on it?"

or, slightly more sophisticated:

"Which one will you choose first?"

Even better, you can turn objections into a framework that gives the child a sense of choice:

"So.... what I'm hearing is that there are three things that are stopping you from getting on with your homework straight away : you're hungry; you've lost your pencil and you need to ask your friend which questions were set for tonight. Which of these will you fix first, I wonder. Obviously, you can't do all three at the same time, so choose one first and then when that's done, move onto the second...... and then the third."

TIP : Be careful to not over use this technique with young children because it will lose its effect.

16. THE "YES" WEEKEND

Parents can easily fall into the trap of continually saying 'no' to their children, especially if their parenting style is one of near continuous fire-fighting. As an experiment, have a *Yes* weekend.

This idea does not mean you'll be letting your kids have free reign of the house to do as they please. It will mean you avoid saying 'no' and other negative words such as 'don't'. Imagine that your children are guests who have come to stay for the weekend – you wouldn't speak to them in the same way that you speak to your children, would you?

What to say instead of 'no' and 'don't':

Child: *"I want an ice-cream now."*

Instead of replying 'NO':

Adult: *"Yes, I know you love eating ice-cream and so do I. We can have some when we get home after our tea. What's your favourite flavour by the way? Mine's strawberry.*

Child: *"Can we go to the park now?"*

Instead of replying 'NO':

Adult: *"Yes, we can go to the park – after we've had lunch and been to the shops."*

Child: *"I don't want to go home now. Can't we stay longer?"*

Instead of replying 'NO':

Adult: *"I can see if it were up to you, we'd stay here all day. It's hard to leave a place that you enjoy so much."*

You can then save the word 'no' for emergency situations that genuinely require it eg: *"NO, you can't pretend to be Superman and jump out of the window!"*

17. YES SET

Here's a very clever way of getting your child to say 'yes'. This is a common language pattern that you'll see used in many advertisements. You might have seen something like this:

- Do you suffer from tiresome back pain?
- Does the constant aching stop you from enjoying life?
- Are you exhausted because you long for a good night's sleep? *followed by:*
- Would you like to learn about our new magical cure?

The pattern starts by asking three questions that will elicit a series of 'YES' responses. Automatically, the mind will flip to giving a positive response to the 4th question.

Choose your 4th question carefully and you'll get your child to agree to what it is you want.

- *So you've been struggling with your maths homework?* YES
- *And you'd like to find a way of making it easier?* YES
- *And making it easier would lead to better marks, wouldn't it?* YES
- *So keeping your files and paperwork in a more organised fashion would do this, wouldn't it?* YES

OR

- *So you're feeling concerned about your weight?* YES
- *You'd like to have more energy and feel fitter?* YES
- *And be able to wear your narrow jeans comfortably?* YES
- *So cutting out crisps and fizzy drinks, would be a step in the right direction?* YES

OR

- *So you're struggling to get to sleep at night?* YES
- *And you wish you could just curl up and drop off easily?* YES
- *And wake up in the mornings feeling refreshed with more energy?* YES
- *So, switching off the computer off earlier would help you do this?* YES

18. GIVE A REASON

Children are far more likely to do as they're told if they are given some understanding of why it is being asked of them. This has been backed by numerous studies that show you are much more likely to get compliance if you give a reason for your request. The reason doesn't need to be detailed and complex, in fact it can be fairly simple. The important thing is not to leave a request just hanging there with a empty space after it; your child will fill it and it may not always be the response you were hoping for.

Imagine you're in a queue, waiting to pay for your shopping. Someone comes up to you and asks if they can jump the queue, saying: *"Can I pay for my items ahead of you?"*

You'll probably be thinking: *"No, get lost… I was here first… why should I let you in…"* or words to that effect.

Now, imagine that same person comes up to you and says: *"Can I pay for my items ahead of you… BECAUSE… I got held up and now I'm running really late for my appointment."*

This kind of statement is much more likely to elicit a 'YES' response from you. But think about it: why should it? It's not your fault the person is running late. It's only a feeble reason: it's not as if anyone has died or is in danger. The person is simply running late.

But it works! It becomes much harder to reject the request when a reason is given. Test it out.

"Can you help me carry the shopping from the car ...BECAUSE... there are just too many bags for me to do them in one trip."

"Can you put your shoes away in the cupboard please ...BECAUSE... they're getting scuffed each time someone walks past."

"Can you leave your mobile phone in the basket on the hall table at dinner time ...BECAUSE...I have something I want to show you as we eat."

"Please can you tidy your things away from the sitting room ... BECAUSE... we all feel happier when the house looks nice."

19. CAUSE AND EFFECT

In a similar vein to giving a reason, you're more likely to get compliance if you highlight the effect of doing something:

X will make Y

A can help B

"Laying out your school clothes the night before WILL HELP you to be ready more quickly in the morning."

"Being organised and packing your school bag the night before WILL HELP you to feel more relaxed at the end of the day."

"Taking nice long slow breaths when you're in the exam room CAN HELP you feel more relaxed."

20. USE *OPEN* AND *CLOSED* QUESTIONS APPROPRIATELY

Closed questions are ones that begin with:
Will you? / Can you? / Did you? / Have you? / Are you?

These are more likely to receive simple 'yes' or 'no' answers. They can end a communication cycle and stop a conversation in its tracks.

Open questions, on the other hand, use words such as:
How? / What? / Why? / When? / With whom?

They are much more likely to receive a fuller answer with more information.

"Did you have a good day at school? vs What did you do at school today?"

"Have you finished your homework? vs When will you finish your homework?"

"Are you hungry? vs What would you like for lunch?"

21. IT'S / LET'S / THAT IS

This has to be one of my favourite ways to start a sentence and you'll probably notice this pattern many times as I use it throughout the book. This is referred to as the 'lost performative'. It means the original source of authority or speaker is lost.

It's a great way to introduce a suggestion:

It's possible to… (Who says? It's deliberately vague.)

It's only natural that… (According to who?)

It's always a good idea… to tidy your desk before starting your homework (two clever words in one sentence).

Let's see how quickly we can clear away these toys (rather than *tidy up this mess*).

That is a great idea… and the more you think like that…

*It's good that **you're starting** to realise* (lost performative and presupposition)

Some people … find that it's easier to do it quickly.

22. LIKE YOU

The 'Like You' pattern is useful for slipping into conversations and can boost your child's self-esteem and establish rapport.

I, like you…… is received as I like you……

For example:

I, like you, understand how important it is to have some time out with your friends.

I like you, completely get how nice it is to eat sweet, sugary foods… and that's why we'll be baking a lovely big chocolate cake on Sunday.

I, like you, realise that you have lots of choices in front of you…

I was talking to one of the other kids at school… like yourself… who said that…

And you can flip this phrase around too:

You, like me… will eventually become: You like me…

You, like me … recognise the importance of having a tidy, organised desk.

You, like me... understand the benefits of eating healthy vegetables.

Keep using the 'You, like me' set in a hypnotic voice and notice how things change!

23. REFLECTIVE LISTENING

Help your child to get into the habit of looking for solutions by listening to their complaints or grievances and instead of making placating noises, or (worse) ignoring the complaints altogether, simply reflect or bounce the statement back to them with a positive spin on it.

When your child says: *"It's too hot in here."*

Bounce back with: *"Ah you'd like to feel cooler? What would make you feel better – opening a window or removing your jacket?"*

Or:

Child: *"I hate sharing a bedroom."*

Adult: *"So, you'd like to have some space to yourself? What is it about having your own space that appeals to you?"*

Child: *"The room wouldn't be messy with Lego all over the floor."*

Adult: *"OK – so you'd like your sister to tidy her toys and the floor area to be clear?"*

These responses are less moaning, less complaining and more solution focused.

24. LEADING QUESTIONS

This is a useful language pattern that can take the child from the question being asked, or the statement being made, to the desired solution.

"So, you've been feeling worried about your exams – to make yourself aware that you need to do something more about them?"

"I get it – you've come to the conclusion that you don't like any of the vegetables that we eat at home, in order to start experimenting and tasting some new ones."

"So, you're talking to me about this now – in order to start making some changes?"

"So, you're telling me about how much you hated this year's maths teacher – so you can begin to look forward to the new one you'll be having when you go back to school?"

25. MOVING THINGS FORWARD AND OVERCOMING PROBLEMS

These useful phrases will help your child to shift from focusing on the negative and start visualising a happy outcome for the future:

"I wonder when you'll start becoming aware that you feel different."

"How do you think you'll notice that you feel much better?"

"Hey, how good are things going to be once you've solved this problem?"

"Which of all the new ideas that you're rapidly thinking of, do you think you'll become aware of first?"

"Isn't it nice to know that those happy feelings are becoming more and more a part of your life?"

"And the most amazing thing about struggling to get over a problem is that once you've done it, all of those good, positive feelings will keep moving you forward ..."

"OK, so together we're going to write out a list of ideas – shall we do this right now or later this afternoon?"

26. HELPING YOUR CHILD 'SEE' THE END RESULTS

'Seeing' the end result is a skill that we acquire as we go through life.

We do this automatically and encouraging your children to get into the habit of doing this will spur them on to continuing the task through to a conclusion. They'll be feeling more motivated.

"And now as you begin to tidy your room, notice how you're already starting to get a picture of how good it's going to look when you've finished."
(VISUAL CUE)

"Learning how to play a new piece on the piano can seem like an uphill slog to begin with, but as you practice over and over, you might already be starting to hear the round of applause you'll receive when you perform it at the school concert."
(AUDITORY CUE)

"I know you're not really in the mood for maths homework, but as you begin to fill in the answers, you'll also start thinking about how good it's going to feel when you hand the completed work in tomorrow."
(KINAESTHETIC CUE)

Notice how I adapted the sentences to accommodate different preferences. Listen carefully to the type of language your child uses to see whether they're more 'visual', 'auditory' or 'kinaesthetic'.

For more details on whether your child is a visual, auditory or kinaesthetic learner, see Chapter Seven.

27. MIND READING

Certain phrases imply that you can see into your child's mind and understand what they're going through. This enables you to show empathy, despite the fact that they may not have shared or verbalised their feelings with you yet, if indeed they ever will. It's often the case that children find it difficult to put their feelings into words.

Use phrases such as:

I can see that

I sense that

I understand that

I understand that you're choosing to do what feels just right for you

I wonder what kind of extra help you'd need and how you'd start to use it?

You might start noticing…

You might find that…

You might … experience something good…

28. DELAY THE ANSWER

Don't feel you have to respond to everything that's raised immediately. And certainly, never respond in the heat of the moment when feeling slightly angry.

It's OK to say:

"That's an interesting point. I'm not quite sure what the right answer is here, so I'm going to think about it and we can discuss it some more after that."

29. NO-ONE'S PERFECT

None of us is perfect. We all have melt-downs from time-to-time and make mistakes. If your child kicks off because he can't have an ice-cream say, or he's failed a maths test because he didn't revise enough, don't focus purely on a punishment. It's missing the point because your child needs help with learning from these experiences and help with making better choices next time.

Aim to create a no-blame culture in your family. Rather than it being someone's fault, use the line:

"This isn't working well is it? What shall we do to fix it?"

30. PRAISE BE!

We're all familiar with the concept that we should praise our children frequently in order to build up their self-esteem, encourage them to ditch bad habits and behave well. However, it's not uncommon, to run out of words to use and so most parents, and indeed teachers, find themselves stuck with a limited vocabulary and use words such as:

wonderful

well done

amazing

brilliant

fantastic

clever

As well intentioned as this kind of superlative praise can seem, these words quickly lose their meaning if used too often and end up sounding a little fake. When I ran a Montessori school earlier in my career, I became very aware of this. You can imagine a scenario where 26 children are lining up ready to go home. If the teacher tells each child that the piece of artwork they're taking home is 'fantastic' or 'brilliant', it's going to become obvious to the child that it's an automatic response and not a genuine compliment.

In just the same way, it's not uncommon for parents to end up using these single word expressions in response to a mediocre performance, leaving the child slightly confused and wondering if they are in fact able to do any better.

It's more important to praise the effort and the intention, rather than the outcome as this will increase your child's motivation and the willingness to take on challenges.

Begin by noticing and commenting on exactly what your child has done that is right or just OK. This is literally 'saying what you see'. Below I have included examples of two ways of praising your children. Which one do you think is most effective?

"Wow, your homework is brilliant."

VS

"Even though you weren't sure of some of the answers, I can see that you took the time to answer all the questions on this worksheet. You didn't leave any blanks."

"Your painting is fantastic."

VS

"I can see you used lots of colours in this painting. That's a very interesting shade of blue – did you mix it with white to get it that pale?"

"You ate that mouthful – clever boy, well done."

VS

"I can see that you used your knife and fork and tasted some of your broccoli. That's one of the vegetables that's really good for your body. It has lots of vitamins to help you grow stronger and run faster."

"You are brilliant at laying the table!"

VS

"I can see that you've worked very hard and laid the table neatly – all the knives and forks in the correct place lined up like soldiers. I think you're ready to lay out the glasses. Would you like to pour some drinks too?"

This kind of dialogue will immediately show your child that you're paying attention and noticing what he's doing. This is a much better way of engaging your child and elevating their feelings of confidence.

The concept of saying what you see also improves behaviour and can be used in a variety of circumstances. Practice makes perfect, but if you are unsure of where to begin, follow this three step plan:

1. Notice a little thing that your child is doing right – even if it is only the smallest step in the right direction.

2. Tell your child exactly what you notice. Describe the behaviour in detail.

3. Leave out the over-the-top superlatives.

Just to help you, I've included the following sentence starters:

You've been remembering to…

I hear you...

In the past week, you...

Nowadays you usually...

I can see that you...

31. GETTING MORE OF THE BEHAVIOUR YOU WANT

Now you're getting the knack of it, think carefully about all the times you fall back on bland, automatic praise. However, well intentioned it may be, it can be confusing your child and contributing to their negative behaviour. Imagine all the different scenarios where saying what you see would be much more effective:

"You've already got your underwear and one sock on! You're almost halfway dressed."

"I noticed that you put one of your sweet wrappers in the bin."

"Ah, I told you it was time for bed and you came up to the bathroom straightaway."

"You're remembering to eat with your mouth closed – that's polite."

"It's nice and happy round the table today – the grumpy faces have vanished."

"You remembered to play quietly whilst I was on the telephone."

"You've stopped whingeing. Now I want to listen to you."

TIP: It's best to use these 'descriptive praise' methods for situations that are changing in a positive way. It will feel slightly insulting if you keep slipping it into your conversations to praise things your child can already do.

32. WORDS AND PHRASES THAT DON'T WORK

There won't be a parent in the land who hasn't from time-to-time, wished they hadn't made that put-down remark to their kids. Without even thinking, those words sometimes just spill out of our mouths.

Think back to your own childhood and recall some of the remarks your parents made to you. And remember how they made you feel.

The phrases that I particularly dislike are those that are followed with the line: *'Oh, I was only joking'* or *'I didn't mean it – can't you take a joke*? 'Jokes' like this are never particularly funny. However flippantly a comment may be said they do damage. Over time your child will be drip-fed a diet of put-down comments that will dent their self-image.

To end this section and before we move onto the specifics, let's just pause for a moment and consider some words that definitely do not work. These are probably all the same words and phrases your parents once said to you, which you found utterly infuriating, yet inexplicably you now find yourself saying to your kids.

Examples might include such classics as:

- *Father Christmas won't bring you any presents.*
  I once overheard a parent threatening her child with this punishment in August! The likelihood of her following through some four months later is pretty slim. The misdemeanour will have been forgotten but the fact that Mum 'lied' won't have been. It's the quickest way to lose credibility.

- *You're grounded.*
  Imprisonment never made anyone feel good and if you're hoping your child learns from their mistakes and makes amends, they won't. They need to be in a good and resourceful state of mind to change their behaviour.

- *Because I said so.*
  This is a classic statement from my own childhood. It doesn't really explain anything and demotes the child to a second-class citizen.

- *It's MY house, so I make the rules.* Or *When you live in your own house, you can do what you want.*
  A surefire way of making your child feel like a temporary lodger. Why should they care for their environment if it doesn't belong to them? It may be your 'house' but it's their family 'home' too, remember.

- *How many times do I have to keep telling you NOT to leave your shoes there?*
  Well, where would you like me to leave my shoes, Mum and Dad? Tell me, show me and perhaps I'll be able to do it! Too often we tell our children what NOT to do rather than getting clear on what it is we want.

- *Why do you always have to let me down?*
  Meanwhile, the child is wondering why, Mum and Dad, do you have to embarrass me?

- *Why can't you make me feel proud of you, just for once?*
  Ditto

Here are some more words and phrases that might sound familiar. My recommendation is never use them – there are better ways to speak to your family.

- *Kids nowadays*
- *Your generation*
- *Things were better in my day*
- *We had it tough – you don't realise how lucky you are*
- *Can't you do anything right?*
- *Moan, moan, moan, that's all you ever do.*
- *You never listen to a word I say*

- *You can't sit still for one minute*
- *Everyone else seems to manage*
- *There are starving poor children in Africa*
- *You're just like your father*
- *Your sister can do it, so why can't you?*
- *You're behaving like a baby*
- *Anyone would think you're a toddler*
- *Think yourself so clever do you?*
- *It was good enough for me when I was growing up*
- *What makes you think you're so special?*
- *What's the matter with you?*
- *Trust you to be the trouble-maker*
- *I know what you're like*
- *You're just plain bone idle*
- *The trouble with you is..*
- *Face it, you're just not good at maths and never will be*
- *I couldn't do maths at school either*
- *I suppose that's what you call clever, is it?*
- *Children should be seen and not heard*
- *See how many grey hairs you're giving me*
- *Mum's got enough on her plate without you adding to her woes*
- *Look what you've made me do*
- *You'll never amount to much*
- *You'll grow up to regret this when you can't get a job*
- *Don't come crying to me when you're unemployed and miserable*
- *Can't you hurry up?*
- *I haven't got all day, you know.*
- *Do you have to be so clumsy / careless /stupid!*

Turn your comments round and use words that will boost your child's self esteem, such as:

- *I love being with you and us spending time together*
- *I felt so proud of you…*
- *You make me really proud to be your Mum/Dad/teacher*
- *I really care about you*
- *You are really very special…*

- *You're such fun to be with*
- *You're a really good friend – it's good to see you take care of others*
- *Look at you – all smartly dressed – you have a good eye for colour*
- *I really value your opinion*
- *What do you think?*
- *I trust you*
- *I have every faith in you*
- *You're a star*
- *I love your smile*
- *I can accept that you're cross with me*
- *It's OK for you to make mistakes*
- *There are times when I get mad with you but I still love you because*
- *I know that you can be short-tempered at times, but I also know that…*

33. PUTTING IT INTO PRACTICE

In the next section, I'll be showing you how to apply the words and language patterns that you've learnt so far, to ordinary everyday situations that anyone raising or working with children faces. So stay patient for the moment – my aim is to help you become a successful communicator and there's much more to learn……

SECTION TWO

WORDS IN ACTION

3

Day-to-Day Tantrums, Rows & Flare-Ups

In this section, I'll be tackling the three main areas that seem to cause families a great deal of stress – sibling fights; tantrums in the supermarket and arguments over screen time. Of course there are many more issues that can cause flare-ups – and reading through these sections will enable you to pick up some valuable tips to apply to your own particular problem.

However, it's a fact that parents and children who feel more connected, have fewer disagreements and falling outs. Children take notice of people that they feel connected to – so if your children aren't listening or co-operating, you need to strengthen those feelings of connection with more special one-to-one time.

I accept that if you're a busy parent who's holding down a job, organising a home and having to share yourself across two or more children, time is going to be tight. But rather than assuming this is unachievable, it's time to get creative and start thinking about how to introduce special moments into ordinary day-to-day living.

I'm really not a great believer in taking children out for special treats in order to bond and get that one-to-one time. It can feel so fake. Your child knows if things haven't been going well between you both and when you suddenly dive in and say *"Hey, I was thinking – how about we go and get a pizza together at the weekend?"* your child will be suspicious. It will feel odd and he'll start wondering why you're doing this and will worry. When anxiety starts to kick in, your child will start playing up a little. Don't be surprised if when you do go out, he's off his food, moans a bit and wants to go straight back home.

The scenario is too intense for him and you'll be left thinking that your child never appreciates what you do for him. *"I try to be nice and take him out for a pizza and all he does is complain. He's so ungrateful!"*

No – he's not ungrateful but he felt uncomfortable and his 'fight or flight' automatic response took over. Save your money and get one-to-one time at home.

Getting time together and developing a connection without making a big deal of it:

- Help your child tidy their bedroom. Getting on the floor with them and helping them to sort toys or fold clothes can be valuable bonding time for you both. They'll appreciate you making an effort for them and it will come across as a true sign of caring, especially if you say something such as *"Now that the room's tidy, it will be so much easier for you to do your homework here, won't it?"* or *"This will make it easier for you to find things in the morning when we're all in a rush, won't it? I like knowing that things are neat and tidy for you."*

- Let them know you're thinking about them and their needs *"How about I pick up some more lined paper for you while you're at school today. Do you want just one pad or more? And what about a new ruler – I noticed yours got broken the other day."* Bliss – who doesn't like feeling cared for?

- On a one-to-one car journey, be interested in the music that they like and let them play it (loudly) on the CD player in the car, so you can hear it too – rather than simply letting them plug themselves into their mp3 players. Have a conversation about the music and ask questions.

- Look through family photos – the 'selfie' generation love looking at pictures of themselves. Select a few images that you both feature in – this will act as a reminder of your relationship and the deep bond you have. It goes much deeper than last Tuesday's argument over who was supposed to be doing the washing-up.

- Laugh together. As much as it may pain you to watch their choice of movies and TV shows, spending time in each other's company with happy feel-good endorphins fizzing round you both, will break the cycle and feeling of not getting along together. You don't need to say anything, just share a good moment.

- Care for a family pet together – clean the hamster cage, bath or walk the dog. Too often I hear families moaning about whose pet it is – *"it's your bloomin' hamster, you asked for it and you can clean it out"* or moaning about who's going to walk the dog, rather than realising that you could all do it together.

Remember, all these examples are ways that you could factor extra 'together' time into your daily routine without making it a big deal of it. As soon as you have to start making a special effort to do it, you'll never find enough time.

GETTING SOME PEACE AND QUIET:

"I'd just like some peace and quiet!" is a phrase that's often used by parents, but as we all know, children's natural exuberance and energy can regularly mean that the house is anything but peaceful and certainly not quiet!

When kids are making lots of noise, it's usual for Mums and Dads to start raising their voices too. They have to - just to get their requests heard. But as many of you will have discovered, the louder you get, the louder the children get too! The tone and volume of your voice starts to lead the kids in the wrong direction. Before you know it, getting any kind of "peace and quiet" in the house seems a distinct impossibility.

Follow these tips and see what a difference it can make.

1. There's a great NLP technique called **"Matching, Pacing & Leading"** that will help: Start by matching the tone of your voice with theirs, even if you just say something like *"whoa, there's a lot of excitement today, isn't there?"*, in quite a loud voice. Keep this up for a few moments so that you *'fall into step'* with them. Then gradually start altering the tone and speed of your own voice. Start slowing down, lower your tone and begin to speak more quietly and you'll notice that the kids gradually start matching you and your behaviour – you'll be *'leading'* them in a different direction.

2. You can tell the kids to **"be quiet"** – but what exactly do you mean? Your child may not know or completely understand. Is it total silence that you're after or just less noise and running around? Be more specific in your request and you're more likely to get a result. Give an example of a time when they were quiet and ask them to see if they could be just like that. Eg. *"Let's see if we can be quieter – just like we were yesterday, when everyone came home from school, crept onto the sofa and curled up as quiet as tiny little mice."*

3. **Give a reason** – if you explain why you're asking for something, your wish is more likely to be granted. For example: *"Let's turn the volume down and start being a bit quieter because we need to decide what we're going to do next and it will be easier to think of good ideas"*. A phrase like this may sound a bit vague but that's deliberate. The vagueness will cause temporary confusion in your child's mind and stop them in their tracks. Saying something like *"let's be quiet because the baby's sleeping"* won't have the same effect. In fact, you may have already discovered that it can make things worse!

4. **Say 'thank you'** – we're used to thanking people *after* they've done something for us, but what about thanking *before* it's been done? I've often seen this work really well because children

naturally want to please people, especially their parents. So next time you ask your child to wash their hands, come to the table, switch off the TV, quickly follow it up with a *"thank you, that's so helpful of you"*. It's a great way to wrong-foot a child who was going to ignore your request – once they've been thanked, they feel obligated to perform the task.

These tips are a more effective way of creating a change in behaviour – without needing to shout and yell. This reminds me of my days as a Montessori Teacher – whenever my classroom got way too noisy, I'd start *whispering*. The exact opposite of what you'd think I'd need to do.

It can take a bit of courage to do this, because as a teacher you need to gain control of a large group of unruly children quickly – and it's natural to think you need to shout to restore order. But you have to trust that the process will work. Kids are naturally curious and they'll want to hear what you're saying and will lower their voices very quickly so that they can hear you. A surprising, but very effective way to get some well-deserved **"peace and quiet"**.

GETTING KIDS TO TIDY UP:

If you struggle to get your children to tidy up after themselves – and let's face it, who doesn't - then it's very likely that you've fallen into the trap of using the following phrases:

"Do you have to leave the room in such a mess?"
"Don't leave the room in a mess!"
"How many times have I told you not to leave the room in a mess?"

As you'll have already discovered, the situation never seems to improve. The problem here is there are lots of references to messy rooms and none that talk about tidy ones.

Remember this:

Your words are always creating those pictures or images inside your child's mind. Each time you say 'Don't leave the room in a mess', a picture of a messy room is what they'll get. It's really difficult to then make the room look tidy, because they're looking at the wrong 'picture' or image in their mind.

It's a bit like having a jig-saw puzzle – imagine all the pieces are scattered on the floor in front of you and then someone gives you the lid of the box so you can look at the picture and assemble the puzzle correctly. Only, the picture they've given you is the wrong one! It's going to be a struggle to put it together, isn't it? The same kind of thing happens inside your child's mind – without realising it, you're confusing things for them.

It is much better to say:

"Let's leave the room looking nice and tidy."
Then be more specific:
"Let's put all the Lego back in the tub and the pencils back in the cupboard."
Give an example of when this was done before:
"Just like you did yesterday evening. Do you remember? The room looked fabulous afterwards."

TIP:

Take photos of the room when it's all tidied up and stick them onto a piece of large A4 card and keep it as a reference somewhere in the room.

"Let's see if we can make the room look like this again. (Point to the photograph) Can you see? All the puzzles are neatly stacked in the corner."

If a child begins to behave in a 'naughty' manner, say, throwing pencils around the floor take the following approach:

- Offer to help:

"I can see you're struggling to put the pencils away in the pot. Perhaps I can help you. How about I put all the blue ones in the pot first. Then you can put a different colour in. Which one would you like to do first, the red or the green?"

- Encourage an older sibling to help with the tidying.

" I can see that you're struggling to put the felt-tipped pens back in their case. Sophie, I wonder if you could help your little sister. I know that you're really good at putting the lids back on the pens. Perhaps you could show her how?"

Don't be surprised if the younger one suddenly finds herself very able to put them all away by herself, thank you very much!

SIBLING RIVALRY

It may drive you mad, but kids fight. It's natural. They fight because they are bored, or they want attention, or because they are angry about something and don't know how to express it, or because life is just plain unfair. You're very unlikely to stop the fights completely. However, the techniques you use to resolve the conflict can make all the difference in the world, both to your own stress levels and how your kids feel about each other and the world in general.

You may be wondering if you should just let them get on with it: sort out their own battles, if you like. There are arguments in favour of this, especially when a badly judged intervention causes more conflict than it solves. Parents that 'take sides' only inflame the situation that in turn can lead to retaliations. However, the other side to this argument is: if you leave matters as they stand, one child might be able to get away with persistent bullying of another. Turning a blind eye is not a viable strategy.

So, what should you do? Well, as with many strategies in this book, it helps if you have prepared beforehand. Kneejerk reactions such as instant punishments, time-out, or attempts to apportion blame will only backfire. Punishing both children regardless is just as ineffective. In fact, I would avoid punishments altogether. They simply spread the negativity.

The best strategy to adopt is to accept and acknowledge each child's feelings and point of view and help them to express it to their sibling.

If at all possible, ignore the fight altogether at the time and bring it up properly at the next Family Meeting (you'll read more about this in Chapter 11). Encourage your children to work together to come to a solution that they agree on and, if necessary prompt them with ideas on how to do that.

If a squabble becomes so severe you absolutely have to intervene immediately, do so, but be utterly direct. This is not the time to ask vague questions such as:

"How many times have I told you not to do that?"

In fact, I'd call out "let's stop". I've created a 'Magic Stop Button' technique that will help here.

Exercise – The Magic Stop Button

You will need paper and coloured crayons and a quiet space where you can sit on the floor comfortably with your child. Work with each of your children individually, so you can give them your full attention.

Say:

"I've been thinking. I know that sometimes it's hard for us to always do the right thing at the right time. Sometimes we start to do things that we later wish

we hadn't. (give examples) *Remember the day your brother's Lego got kicked all over the floor and that made everyone unhappy, didn't it? Or the day that your little sister got hit over the head and we all ended up being cross with each other?"*

(Note: the situation is described in a general way rather than an accusation being made against the child whose fault it was.)

"I know I didn't like shouting at everyone on that particular day, but I just felt cross and couldn't help myself.

Well, I've been thinking. Wouldn't it be a great idea if we could create a special STOP button in our minds, that we could press in an emergency, whenever we found ourselves doing things that we know we shouldn't be doing? Because I know that sometimes, when we feel tired, cross or angry we can't seem to stop ourselves from doing things that we don't want to be doing."

Take 5-10 minutes over the following activity.

1) This should be a calm, peaceful activity so draw your child's attention to the moment by asking them to pretend that they're very gently blowing bubbles through an imaginary wand. You can do this with them.

2) Each time they slowly blow a long breath out, their bodies will automatically ensure that they take a deep breath back in again.

3) Do this several times and you'll notice that the rhythm of the in/out breathing will help to calm and relax them.

4) Next – explain that you'll both be designing a magic STOP button. An imaginary button inside your mind that can be pressed quickly to stop any unwanted behaviours.

5) Ask your child to close their eyes and take a few moments to imagine what their special, magic button could look like.

6) Give prompts to help your child with their design. *"Now, I don't know if your button will be a round button, a square button or maybe even a triangular button. But I do know that you'll be able to start seeing it clearly now."*

7) *"And how about the colour? I don't know if you're going to choose a red button, a blue button, green or even yellow or orange. I wonder what colour you'll be thinking of."*

8) Continue to gently guide your child in their design, ensuring that they have plenty of time to dream and imagine. Encourage them to tell you out-loud what it is that they're seeing and make a note of the details that they give you.

9) Then you can ask them to open their eyes and now draw a picture of the button that they visualised in their mind.

10) Sit with them as they draw their picture – and perhaps you'll want to draw one for yourself too.

11) When the drawings are finished, explain to your child that next time they feel cross or angry, all they'll need to do to stop feeling bad, is press the magic STOP button.

12) Practise now – ask your child to close their eyes once more and imagine pressing that STOP button hard. Could they do it?

13) Let's test it out again. Ask your child to run across the room. And when you call out 'Let's STOP!' ask them to press their imaginary button and see how quickly their bodies stop for them. It's like an emergency stop – slamming the brakes on quickly.

14) When you've tested it out a few times and your child is happy, stick the picture up on the wall or fridge where it can be seen.

15) With this visual image in his mind, your child will find it very much easier to gain control over his emotions and body.

16) In the future, each time you see your child in the throes of doing something they shouldn't be doing, just call out 'Let's STOP!' This should come as a friendly command rather than a telling off.

Note: if at any time in the future you find the STOP button doesn't work, then it's a case of going back to the drawing board. Tell your child that the button needs fixing. During the visualisation process, guide them with their changes – along the lines of:

- *Would it be better if the button were bigger?*
- *Perhaps you need to change the shape?*
- *What about the colour – would you like to change this at all?*
- *How about turning the button into a handle or lever that you pull down instead?*
- *Would it be better if it made a sound?*
- *How about the sound of a ship's foghorn or a cow mooing? Or a voice shouting STOP? And if so, whose voice? A super-hero perhaps?*
- *You can research some sounds and voices on the internet and ask your child to choose one.*

You can allow your child to have some 'practise' using the new button – running around the garden for example and doing an emergency stop each time you call out 'Let's STOP!'

The image of their magic button will come into their minds at the same time, helping them to take greater control over their body.

Once they have ceased the unwanted behaviour, such as picking fights with siblings, praise them for it: *"You realised that it wasn't a good idea to do that and you managed to stop yourself from continuing, really FAST. You're gaining control, all the time, aren't you?"*

Get down to your child's level: One of the first things I recommend to parents who are faced with a major sibling conflict is to get down to your children's level to connect with them, rather than standing and towering over them. During an argument, anxiety levels will be high and an adult getting cross or talking from a great height will add to this.

Go to the injured party first: If there is an obviously injured party, go to them first and soothe them. This will ensure that the naughty one doesn't get immediate attention for his behaviour. If you launch into a heated lecture, he will start learning that the best way to engage with an adult is to fight with his siblings.

Secondly, as you start to soothe, hug and reassure the injured one, it'll give you a few valuable moments of breathing space to soothe and calm yourself down too. Take a deep breath before tackling the unwanted behaviour. If you shout and lash out, you'll be demonstrating exactly the kind of behaviour you want to stop and you won't be a good teacher.

Thirdly, by attending to the injured one first, you also have the opportunity to 'include' the naughty one in the soothing process – they could perhaps fetch some sticking plasters, a cold flannel or a drink of water – rather than excluding them, which is not what they really need at this point.

Don't insist on an apology: Once you have calmed the situation down, don't drag an apology out. Your children will be feeling unhappy, cross and angry and need help, support and guidance. Now is not the time to insist one or other of them says 'sorry'. They feel confused and absolutely not sorry at all right at this precise moment. If you make a child apologise when they don't genuinely feel it, you'll be teaching them to lie.

It is far better to include an 'apology' section in your Family Conference or Meeting. Lead by example and apologise for your own behaviour:

"I'm really sorry I got shirty with you guys when we were getting in the car the other day. It was just that I was worried we'd be really late for school. As it turned out, we were on time, so I needn't have worried so much. I'll remember that next time."

Again, don't force an apology out of your children. Simply demonstrate that this is part and parcel of normal family life. Little by little, they'll get the message that it makes everyone feel better to say sorry.

Encourage bonding: There are lots of techniques you can use to strengthen the bonds between siblings, so they are not so inclined to argue. You could, for example, play 'kids versus parents' games. Whilst it's common to see families divide themselves up into teams by spreading the children evenly between the adults to 'balance' things out, it doesn't help them form a strong unit. Choose different kinds of games that will suit their abilities. Children can chase parents round the garden, play hide and seek, or Twister, and not be disadvantaged.

Work hard to constantly reinforce the idea that your siblings love each other and get along well. Take photographs of them playing together, having fun and stick them into a small photo album to look at on a regular basis. Looking through photo albums can even take the place of a bedtime story. Encourage your children to tell the story of what was happening in the picture.
Use words and phrases such as:

"I can see you're sharing your toys today – that's kind."

"Playing together again. That's good fun isn't it?"

Beware the self-fulfilling prophecy: Avoid talking about your children as siblings who 'always fight' and 'just can't get along'. Too many of us greet our partners and other family members at the end of a busy day with 'bad news' and stories of fights and arguments. Save those stories for another time. When your children are in earshot, deliberately start talking about how their behaviour is improving and how well they seem to be getting along these days. Even if your children are not in the same room as you, they'll be listening and absorbing your every word. And remember, your words are busily creating their self-image. The sooner they can start to see themselves as siblings who get along, the sooner that's what they'll become.

WORDS THAT WORK

Remind yourself that any child that repeatedly hits their brother or sister is not feeling good on the inside and they will need help too. Begin your conversation by saying something like:

"I bet you were feeling bad on the inside to have done that. Let's take a few moments to sit down and think about what the problem is."

Remember to 'reframe' any complaints that come out of this conversation (Refer to the Words that Work chapter). For example:

"She's in the way of my puzzles."

Would get the response:

"Oh I see, you'd like her to move and give you more space to build your jig-saw? Let's think about how we could ask her to do this for us".

It is always worth bearing in mind the reason given for an outburst may not be the real reason. Children struggle to put their feelings into words and will point to the first thing in their line of sight and say:

"It's you! You're the reason I'm feeling so bad!"

Actually, many adults do exactly the same, so it's worth keeping this in the back of your mind and noticing if you fall into the same trap.

TIP : Sniff the baby. This may seem like a weird tip, but if you're worried about how your older sibling will respond to the arrival of a new born baby, encourage them to sniff baby's head regularly. Researchers have discovered that new-born babies release pheromones from the top of their heads. Regular sniffing of this chemical release will calm down any aggressive instincts your child may have towards a new-born sibling and he'll become more protective instead.

SUPERMARKET TANTRUMS

If your nightmare scenario is supermarket tantrums, don't worry, you are not alone. Trips to the supermarket with children in tow, comes high on the list of things most parents dread

Children get bored very easily and start to whinge and whine. Most parents try to cope by doing their best 'Family Entertainer' impersonation for as long as they possibly can, whilst also dreaming up healthy, interesting meals that will satisfy the whole family and avoid those tantrums round the dinner table. When that fails, the next tactic is to give in and buy the kids a sticky bun to eat. As we all know, that keeps them happy for the 15 seconds it takes them to polish off the bun and then you're back to square one. At the checkout, there's another meltdown accompanied by requests for the sweets that are cleverly placed in the very, very narrow checkout aisle.

The key to getting out of this routine is to plan in advance and here are a few things you can do to 'train' your child to behave as you would like them to:

1. Create a Shopping book. You'll need an exercise book, a glue stick and some scissors.

Just as you have a shopping list, encourage your kids to compile their own 'shopping books' as a reference or guide. They can fill this book with pictures of the products that you'll be buying when you next go shopping. They can draw pictures, or cut pictures out of magazines or supermarket promotional material. Take labels off tins as you use them at home and let them stick them in their book. Cut small bits of cereal packets and other packaging and let them stick those in the book too.

Now, when you're shopping you can play a matching and sorting game. This is a form of early mathematics. To keep your child occupied you can ask them to look out for things that are on your shopping list and refer to the exact branding in their reference books. They can match the label in their book to the item on the shelf.

2. **Share your shopping list**. Draw tick boxes on the list and each time an item goes in the basket, ask your child to tick it off. This helps to make it clear to the child that you know exactly what you've come shopping for and by sharing your list, you'll both feel more connected. It's team work.

3. **Stick rigidly to the list**. If you're hoping to wean your children off making those tiring demands for sweets and toys, then you must lead by example. Only buy those things that are on your list. If you start to deviate from the plan after getting distracted by other promotional items, your child will hear you say 'I think I'll just take one of those too. Oh yes, and I fancy that today.' It's no wonder that they copy and randomly pick items off the shelves too. When you get cross and tell them to put it back on the shelf, they get upset and not surprisingly. It's not fair! You're doing it and young children are all programmed to copy their parents. They just want to join in.

It may be irritating if you've forgotten to put something on your list because this strategy will mean that you've got to walk past the item, knowing that you'll have to wait till next time. But, if you're really keen to have better behaved kids in the supermarket, stick with this and follow the plan to the letter.

4. **Keep it short**. Our supermarkets keep growing in size. It's not

uncommon now to find pharmacies, opticians, cafés and electronics sections. A quick trip to the shop can take two hours. Using your new strategy, make your supermarket visit just five or 10 minutes. Tell your child you're just going in to get two items. Go in, look for them, go to the checkout, get your child to pay, pack and go.

Throughout the visit use lots of descriptive praise:

"You're being very helpful today."

"I really appreciate you helping me find the milk."

The aim is to make your child feel successful. Repeat this process two or three times and then gradually lengthen the time to 15 minutes or half an hour. Building up slowly, will enable you to gather lots of proof and evidence that supermarket trips are manageable and your child's self-image will gradually change.

5. **Pick a different supermarket.** If something happens often enough, we begin to 'anchor' a set of emotional feelings to it. This could be a sound, a smell, a taste or some other experience. We all know people who feel weak at the knees when they come across 'that hospital smell', or the sight of a needle, or the mere mention of the dentist. Nothing needs to have happened yet, but they'll already start feeling bad. Bad feelings will have been attached or 'anchored' to those experiences.

If your child has repeatedly behaved badly in your local supermarket and been told off each time, perhaps even crying and screaming, then they'll only need to see the logo above the front door to already be feeling bad. And, more than likely, you'll be feeling the same way. You'll both remember last week's embarrassing meltdown and sure enough, the same thing's going to happen over and over again. It's a self-fulfilling prophecy and you'll end up going home saying to yourself; *"I knew that was going to happen. I knew I couldn't trust you to behave!"*

You're both locked into the same pattern of behaviour because there are simply too many reminders around you.

If you want to break the cycle of behaviour, it's best to start with a clean slate. Introduce a new regime. Choose a new supermarket and start afresh with different branding, different colours and different behaviour.

You'll enjoy it more too.

SCREEN TIME

It's a question that has sparked a debate among modern parents: how much should you allow your children to use screens? Daily life includes an increasing number of screens, whether it is TV, smartphones or tablets and the chances are, if your child gets half the chance, they'll be glued to theirs most of the time.

For a long time, the advice was to avoid too much exposure to screens. In recent years there has been a shift in thinking and experts now agree there are some advantages to life in a 3-D world, as long as limits are set. And, therein lies the rub. As any parent knows, enforcing these limits is virtually impossible when you are fighting against the lure of a flashy gadget.

The answer is, in fact, quite simple: have a clear set of rules.

If your child were to walk into the house wearing muddy wellingtons before running upstairs and jumping into bed, you'd be cross. You'd tell them off in no uncertain terms. They'd be left in no doubt that this is unacceptable behaviour and they're not allowed to do this again. Muddy wellingtons belong elsewhere. That's the rule!

And yet, when it comes to monitoring and regulating screen time, be it on their mobile phones, tablet devices or laptops, we're flaky. This is probably because we have no sphere of reference. We didn't have such a wide range of technology when we were kids, so we're not really sure what we should be happy with or not.

We all 'feel' they spend far too much time being electronically connected, but on the other hand, we're secretly relieved because it shuts them up when we're driving in the car and gives us time to catch up on doing other things around the house. Perfect babysitters at the press of a button.

And then we feel a bit guilty for being bad parents, so we get cross with our kids and moan at them for being attached to their screens for far too long. Most of the time, of course, we're cross with ourselves. Later on, we feel guilty for having shouted at them for simply doing what all their friends are doing. So, to make up for it, we buy them the latest computer game or tablet device for their birthday. We may even try to make ourselves feel better by saying we are buying the games 'just so they don't feel left out', and besides, 'it's all educational' but the truth is, most of us don't know what to think.

Yet, while we're all a bit wishy-washy with the rules, we find them being broken all the time. Or are they? If we haven't actually decided on a rule then it can't be broken, can it?

Don't delude yourself: moaning at your kids each time they whisk out their mobile phones at the dinner table, is not setting boundaries and rules.

It is up to you, as a family, to decide what is and isn't going to be acceptable. What's going to fit with your family values and suit your children's personalities the best?

Some families choose to set rules according to strict time limits, for example, just two hours screen time a day. Personally though, I believe you're storing up a problem for the future. As technology advances, more and more of your child's education is going to take place on a screen. All a sudden, a half-term school project will eat into their time allocation and the whingeing and whining will start. You'll end up giving in and your child will learn that a good moan is exactly what they need to do in order to get the allocation of time extended.

I'm also of the opinion that the more something is forbidden, the more desirable it becomes. It has a scarcity value. Have you ever tried dieting by cutting out certain foods? The first thing you start craving is the very thing you've chosen to eliminate.

Your child will feel hard done by and they'll always be able to list friends who are allowed unlimited use of their devices. In their mind's eye, you'll be the mean, miserable parent! Inevitably, this soured relationship will creep into other areas of your family life.

If this all sounds as if I'm taking your child's side in this debate, you're probably a little bit right.

I remember the long, lonely hours of my own childhood too well and so I feel that mobile phones and social media are amazing tools for staying in touch with friends. I would have loved it!

Too often we hear that children nowadays are not connecting with their friends 'in the real world' and learning few social skills, but the alternative in my day was exchanging scraps of paper with hastily scrawled phone numbers. If you lost these pieces of paper, your friends were lost too. Even if you did have a number, those on the 'shy' side would hesitate to use it. How much easier is it nowadays to text or join a Facebook group? I find it hard to believe that today's youngsters have fewer social skills; they're the best connected generation there's ever been.

When we criticise today's youngsters for being mono-syllabic, spending all their time locked in their bedrooms, we're assuming that yesterday's children spent their days riding bicycles in the woods and grew into healthy, confident individuals who spoke clearly and politely to adults, sailed through job interviews and never wanted to spend time on their own, doing their own thing. It's not true. It's a nice vision, but it's simply not true.

The mind-set we need to accept is: today's technology is wonderful – but it needs to be used correctly.

With this in mind, here are the rules that I would recommend implementing. Of course, every family is different so you have to find the right ones for you and yours. When you've worked out what they're to be – STICK TO THEM!

1. Not under the age of three and seriously limited for the under sixes. Just because your toddler knows how to use their fingers to scroll through your smart phone does not make them a genius. Similarly, just because your school-age child knows how to work the TV better than you do, doesn't mean they should be permanently glued to it. At this tender age your child's brain is developing and human beings are programmed to adapt to their environment. They need to interact with the 'real' world and not the 'virtual' world. So little information comes through a screen and the information that does come through is visual only. Our senses are the foundation of the human intellect – in other words, what we see, hear, taste, touch and smell is all valuable information that programmes our minds. And this can only happen this effectively at this stage.

Do not worry that other people's children get all the screen time they desire. It's not a competition and your child will not get left behind. Let them develop their intellect first by interacting with their environment because without it, they are stunted. Trust me, your child will be smarter, the longer you keep them away from devices.

Your aim as a parent should be to assist your child's mind to develop as fully and completely as it can. Sitting quietly in the garden, playing with a lump of mud and a couple of ants for half an hour is valuable brain development. Do not let your child miss out on these opportunities.

2. Adopt the same rules as the ones you're insisting your children follow. Once you do allow children screen time, agree on your family guidelines – ones you've selected because they mean healthy, happy living.

For example, it may mean a family rule where there are no mobiles at the dinner table and that they should not be carried around in pockets. However, if you make this rule, then you must do the same. Don't tell your child off for fiddling with his phone, while you are scrolling through yours checking your text messages.

3. Create a family charging station. Allocate a place where everyone can leave their phone and tablet device when they're not in use. Get into a routine of doing this with your own devices and your children will automatically copy you. Kids are programmed to learn by copying the behaviours of those around them – do less nagging and more demonstrating how to behave.

4. Not in the bedroom. It's not uncommon to see children with TVs, DVD players, laptops, mobiles phones and tablet devices all humming along nicely as they charge upstairs for the night. This is seriously bad for their health. Looking at screens an hour or so before bedtime makes it harder to fall asleep and interferes with melatonin production – the hormone that induces sleepiness.

Children need to sleep properly for the sake of their health. For example, studies show much of childhood obesity could be down to lack of sleep. Bad tempered, grumpy, tired children crave sweets and sugar. Stop this happening by making sure they get a good night's, uninterrupted, sleep. Make sure your children understand and accept it is NOT acceptable to go online to chat to friends in the small hours of the morning.

5. Stay well connected with each other. The very fact that every member of the family now has a choice about who to chat to in the evenings – another family member or a friend online – is all the more reason to ensure that you all stay well-connected. Your regular Family Conference or Meeting is going to be all the more important now. You must keep talking to each other.

6. Ensure your child has plenty of hobbies that take them away from the screen. Kids need a balance in their lives. Children who spend hours and hours on the devices have nothing else better to do and are, most likely, just plain bored. Ensure that there is something better. Could you choose a hobby for the whole family to get involved with?

Put aside one night a week for playing after dinner board games / scrabble or charades. Kids love acting and posing so why not encourage them to do it in front of the family?

7. Get outdoors more. Studies show that kids who spend more time outdoors in nature are not only calmer and happier but also have improved sleep patterns, perform better at school and are less likely to fall into the trap of becoming overweight. Choose outdoor activities for the whole family such as riding bikes and having picnics in the park. For older children, what about night-time walks by torchlight to see nocturnal animals and stargaze? Or, if you have a safe place to do so, light a small campfire in the evenings and cook sausages.

All the activities will help you to feel more connected as a family. Better connected families are less likely to fracture, propelling children towards social media addictions.

8. Stay safe – be clear on what's dangerous and unacceptable. Your child needs to be aware of what's appropriate and not appropriate behaviour when going online. Find out what your child's school are doing in terms of education. They'll be far more receptive to receiving and following advice that's given there, than having a parent over-react and become a permanent policeman. Your job is to guide and support and it's better to slip this into general conversation rather than panicking and attempting to install bits of software when you don't know what you're doing.

And if you feel uncomfortable discussing issues such as sexting and the posting of explicit images visit one of the many websites that offer telephone support eg: nspcc.org.uk. You'll be able to discuss this with a trained advisor.

WORDS THAT WORK

- *Let's see if we can leave the room looking nice and tidy.*

- *Let's put all the Lego back in the tub and the pencils back in the cupboard – just like we did yesterday evening. Do you remember? The room looked great afterwards.*

- *I can see you're struggling to put the pencils away in the pot. Perhaps I can help you. How about I put all the blue ones in first and then you can put a different colour in. Which one do you want to choose first – the red or the green?*

- *I know you're not really in the mood for tidying up the playroom but as you begin to put the puzzles back into the cupboard, you'll also start thinking about how good it's going to be to come from school tomorrow and sit in a tidy room. You'll be able to stretch right out on the floor, won't you?*

- *This is will be our family charging station. We'll all be charging our devices here when we sit down to eat our evening meal.*

- *Even though you weren't keen on leaving your mobile in the hall at bedtime, I can see that you managed to remember to do it. That's great – and it will become easier to remember to do it each day.*

- *I understand that kids nowadays want to have their phones with them all the time – but as you quickly start to remember to leave it at the charging station at mealtimes, you'll also see how much more relaxed our family dinners will be.*

- *I can sense that this isn't always easy for you – and you're choosing to do the right thing now.*

- *This is how we ......*

- *The reason we do this is ....*

- *This isn't working well, is it? What shall we do to fix it?*

WORDS THAT DON'T WORK

- *How many times have I told you......*

- *Can't you do as you're told......*

- *Don't do that.....*

- *I've told you once and I won't tell you again!* (I bet you will...)

- *Say sorry!* (The heat of the moment is not a time to be demanding apologies – you'll be teaching your child to lie.)

- *Trust you to be the trouble-maker.*

- *I can't trust you with anything, can I?*

- *You can't keep your hands to yourself for one minute, can you?*

- *You never listen – do you?*

- *Stop making so much noise!*

- *Why do you always have to make so much mess / so much noise?*

- *Other mums and dads don't have to put up with this.*

4

Eliminating Fears and Anxiety

Over the years, I've come across people who have phobias of bananas, zips, big plants and pens that 'click' at the top. As I don't personally fear any of these objects, I'll admit there have been times when I've been tempted to say 'don't be so stupid' or 'pull yourself together'.

Perhaps you've experienced similar feelings when your child has come home with some real or imagined fear. Of course, we all know that simply saying 'pull yourself together' won't work. In fact sometimes, the more someone tells us to 'pull ourselves together', the less likely we are to do it.

Whilst you may not understand the fear, it's important to accept that the *thought* is making your child fearful. It's the mechanics of the thought process that produces the physical feelings of fear, rather than the object itself. Which is just as well, because thought processes can be changed. However I very much doubt that supermarkets will stop selling bananas, plants will stop growing and pens will stop 'clicking'.

Almost everyone, adults and children alike, have experienced the feelings of fear or suffered from anxiety. The difference between older and younger generations is most adults realise these feelings are unreasonable and common-sense can then prevail. Children's minds are not usually developed enough to differentiate between reality and fantasy so they need extra help to overcome their worries.

It's not uncommon for a harmless encounter with a barking dog in the park, for example, to turn into a phobia of all dogs, making it impossible for you to visit the park again without hysterical screaming from your child. Once an idea has got stuck in your child's mind, it can be hard to shift. It's the thought process and pictures in your child's mind that are the problem and need changing, rather than the actual dog in the park.

Experts say modern-day pressures simply add to the problem and children as young as two or three are already showing signs of stress, often thanks to modern competitive parenting techniques. As they grow older, academic worries blight 50 per cent of children and anxiety over exams is now a bigger concern to the younger generation than peer pressure, or the need to find a boyfriend or girlfriend[1].

Many childhood fears are entirely natural and tend to develop at specific ages – in many cases they'll grow out of these fears when they get older. According to the Child Anxiety Network, the following fears are common to particular age groups and considered normal:

0-2 Years – Loud noises, strangers, separation from parents, large objects.

3-6 years – Imaginary things such as ghosts, monsters, the dark, sleeping alone and strange noises.

7-16 years – More realistic fears such as injury, illness, school performance, death and natural disasters.

In recent years, this list has been changing. Worrying news items with threats of terrorism, an endless stream of school exams, packed schedules of after-school activities, family break-up and divorce all contribute to a sense of unease. Even when kids are having 'fun' by playing computer games, they're victims of an adrenaline rush as the primitive 'fight or flight' responses designed to keep us safe from

---

[1]   NSPCC

sabre-toothed tigers get triggered. And because modern-day child is doing nothing more than sitting on the sofa 'relaxing', this cocktail of stress chemicals never quite gets burned off.

Left unchecked, these feelings of worry and generalised anxiety, to give this syndrome its proper name, spill over into all areas of a young child's life, creating fear of the unknown – be it a first day at school, a trip to the doctor or dentist, or even attending a friend's birthday party. The symptoms that all is not well are often easy to spot. Perhaps your child is always irritable or angry, or simply withdrawn from friends and family. They may even develop disorders from changes in appetite, sleeplessness, night terrors, or develop a new set of fears over anything from travel to injections. Their anxiety could manifest itself in other habits such as bedwetting, thumb-sucking, tics or stammers.

The good news is: anxiety disorders are very treatable conditions and most of the things that we worry about never happen, so we tend to exhaust ourselves for nothing.

It's important to help children see that most feelings of fear and anxiety are just that – feelings. The great thing about feelings is that they can be changed.

FOOD FOR THE MIND AND SOUL

While many anxieties and phobias are irrational and unlikely ever to happen, it is well worth considering environmental factors as to why your child might be thinking in this way. Everything from the food they eat, to the amount of exercise they take play a part.

Food: Be aware that certain foods will alter your child's stress and anxiety levels as well as create mood swings. Foods they should be eating include plenty of the following: porridge, brown rice, wholegrain breads, fish, turkey, chicken, cottage cheese, pulses, and fruit and vegetables in general. If your child can eat nuts safely, it's a good idea to keep some handy for snacks in between meals.

Avoid toxins: You should also help your child avoid toxins, such as caffeine. Sure, they may not be drinking coffee or tea, but what about energy drinks which are increasingly popular today? Many contain caffeine. Be aware also of the stimulating effects of sugar which will cause fluctuations in blood sugar levels. This includes natural sugars found in fruit juices and smoothies. The effects are similar to symptoms of anxiety. Indeed, your child may not be anxious at all, just overloaded with sugar.

Exercise: The higher our physical tension levels, the more likely it is that we will experience bouts of anxiety. Regular exercise, of at least 20 minutes each day, even if it is only going for a brisk walk, will soak up excess adrenaline and release endorphins. You may find this is all it takes to reduce your child's anxiety levels down to an acceptable level.

Laughter: Another effective (and enjoyable) antidote to see off worries is good, old fashioned laughter. Learning how to laugh in response to day-to-day problems may not be an obvious choice for most of us, but experts are agreed that it may be the best medicine and the quickest way to change your brain chemistry. Watch funny movies, TV programmes, or tell jokes. Can't think of any? Buy a joke book and take turns to read jokes to each other. Encourage your child to become the 'joker' of the family.

Relaxation: Teach your child relaxation techniques. As we all know, when we are afraid, or anxious, we experience a variety of uncomfortable physical symptoms, such as a racing heart or shortness of breath. These physical sensations can be frightening and this is a large part of what makes anxieties and phobias so distressing.

BREATHING TECHNIQUES:

I'd recommend teaching your child a couple of simple breathing techniques, such as these, so they can always summon up an extra bit of help when they need it.

Exercise – Just Breathe

Anxiety can often lead to shortness of breath. This leads to a pale complexion, sweaty hands and face, tightness in the chest and even giddiness or fainting. These are all classic physical symptoms.

'Take a nice deep breath,' is a traditional response. Indeed, it is a phrase we're probably all familiar with and have heard many times. It seems to make sense to say it. Yet, taking a nice deep breath inwards is precisely what an anxious person doesn't need to do.

Many of the symptoms we've mentioned above are caused by having *too much* 'breath' stuck in the lungs. Anxiety causes us to tense up, so we breathe less deeply. As we continue to tense up, possibly in response to the worsening symptoms, the air becomes trapped in the lungs, exacerbating the feelings of panic.

When you see your child having an attack of anxiety, what you need to do is encourage them to purse their lips and blow out slowly.

Keeping your voice calm and steady, say to them: *"Blow out......* *slowly...... for as long as you possibly can. Nice and slowly... keep* *blowing out."*

This will help the excess air leave the body. There'll be no need to tell the child to breathe back in as our bodies automatically respond and the 'in' breath will come naturally.

When I use this technique with children who come to see me, I often tell them to imagine that they're blowing one of those hand-held windmill toys. You need to keep blowing a steady stream of air to get the sails to spin round. Or, in the same vein, you could ask them to imagine blowing a big, big bubble or blowing a balloon up. You can ask your child to put a hand up to their mouth for this exercise and simply blow, blow, blow.

Practice this exercise with your child to induce feelings of relaxation without waiting for them to become stressed and anxious. In fact, the more that you can practice this, the better they'll start to feel generally as their anxiety levels will start to reduce.

Even better, once they learn this technique they can use it by themselves when waiting to go into an exam classroom, for example. Many of the body's stress chemicals can be found in our breath and the more that can leave your child's body, the more relaxed they'll start to feel. And, as the body starts to relax, the mind will start to feel better too

Exercise – Counting breaths

Here's another breathing technique which might be more suitable for an older child if bubbles and windmills seem a bit young and unsophisticated for them.

1) Ask your child to make themselves comfortable, close their eyes, take a deep breath in and then blow out for as long as they possibly can.

2) As they start blowing out, you can begin to slowly count out loud.1......2......3......4......5...etc. (Take this slowly and steadily as racing along with your counting will put them off.)

3) Ask them to keep their attention on the breathing and not to allow other thoughts to creep into their minds.

4) When your child runs out of puff, they can open their eyes once more.

5) What number did they get to? How many seconds were they able to stretch that blow out for?

6) Now ask them to repeat the process. Close their eyes, breathe in deeply and then blow a long slow breath out again. You do the counting again. This second time around, the aim is to beat the score achieved with the previous blow.

7) When they've run out of puff, record the score. You can make a comment such as *"that was a bit longer wasn't it? First time around you scored eight and now you've been able to blow out till you reached the number ten."*

8) Repeat this process again. Say: *"let's see what number we get to third time around, shall we?"*

To make it easier to get into the higher figures each time, there are a couple of variations to the technique that you can use to help:

a) When they hear you say a number, ask them to *see* it at the same time. Say: *"I wonder what colour and size your numbers will be?"*

b) Ask your child to look out of a window and spot an object in the distance. Tell them to imagine blowing out a long, slow breath until they hit it.

JUST WORRYING

Does trying to come up with answers to constant questions and concerns about things that have never happened and are never likely to happen, simply wear you out?

Endlessly discussing worries can often allow them to become more deeply embedded in your child's psyche. While this book is called 'Words that Work', sometimes words are best avoided. You can easily tie yourself in knots trying to reassure your child and if it's not working, then NO words are better than the WRONG words – a hug or a cuddle might be better.

If your child has got stuck in a cycle of worries, then you might never be able to say the right thing. You'll desperately be trying to formulate answers and reassurances for things that may or may not happen and your child will resolutely keep on going round and round in circles, talking about their fears and concerns.

"Yes, but what happens if I get there and there's no-one to play with?"

or

"What if I have no-one to sit next to?"

These are common worries about the future but none of us has a crystal ball. You don't know what might happen and if you pretend to do so, you could actually make things worse.

You can initially empathise with your child by saying something like:

"Oh yes, I can understand how that makes you feel. You felt a little like that when you went to James's party didn't you? And then you easily found a few friends to play with."

And then, I'd recommend parking the conversation by following this exercise:

The Worry Box

Worries are emotional messages that our mind sends to us, in a sense, to look out for or take care of us. For example: the night before going away on holiday you might receive worries about having your passport and tickets to hand – which is a good thing, because then you can take action and ensure that you won't forget them. Likewise, a worry about an exam will prompt you to do some extra revision.

This is fine provided that it really is possible to take some action but with many worries this isn't always possible, so we get stuck with a niggling thought that there's not much we can do about. Acknowledging receipt of these messages is often all that is needed to make them go away – it's a way of tricking the mind into believing that action has been taken.

1) Find a box. It can be an old shoebox, or a small, attractively decorated one. Include your child in this selection and tell them it can be any sort of box that feels right for them. Explain to your child that this is going to be their personal 'Worry Box'.

2) Put a supply of paper and coloured felt-tip pens inside the box. Each time your child gets stuck in a worrying cycle, ask them to have a think about what might be making them feel like this.

3) Take one of the sheets of paper from the Worry Box and ask your child to choose a coloured pen. Having a good selection of coloured pens is useful because you can ask your child what colour he or she thinks this worry is.

4) Ask them to write down the worry, or draw a picture that represents it.

5) Once they've finished, ask them to fold the piece of paper up and put it into the Worry Box. Put the lid firmly on the box and put it away.

(Hint: it's best to keep this box somewhere out of everyday sight eg. the top of a cupboard. Don't store it in the bedroom and certainly not under the bed, otherwise your child will be sleeping 'on their worries' and not feeling very good about it.)

6) By writing the worry down, they will have sent an important message to the subconscious mind, letting it know that the emotional message has been received loud and clear and that it's been acted upon.

7) Each time another worry begins to aggravate your child, follow the same process. Ask them to write it down, fold up the paper and pop it into the box.

8) Over a surprisingly short space of time, you'll find the worries begin to evaporate and will cease to keep nagging your child.

9) At the end of each week, sit down with your child, open the box and empty out the pieces of paper. Read through the worries together and encourage your child to be as pleasantly surprised as you when you both discover that most of them took care of themselves, without requiring any action from either of you whatsoever.

Remember – most of the things that we worry about never happen!

THE MOVIES OF YOUR MIND

Most parents are familiar with those feelings of exasperation because a child simply won't believe that there isn't 'a crocodile under the bed'. No amount of reassurance will allay a child's fears once they've got an idea lodged in their minds, just as night-lights and bedside lamps rarely remove a 'fear of the dark'.

We know the mind and body are very closely connected, so if your child is experiencing a feeling of fear, it's being triggered by their thoughts – made up of pictures and internal dialogue.

Think back to the last time you watched a scary movie at the cinema or on TV. It didn't matter that you knew it was only make-believe, watching the pictures triggered off palpitations, sweaty palms and anxious feelings. The same is happening to your child when they experience a feeling of fear – it's the pictures in the 'movies of the mind' that are scaring them.

There is a very effective NLP technique that is ideal for helping your child with scary thoughts and nightmares.

The Magic TV Control

1) Find a quiet place where your child can feel relaxed and comfortable. You may find it useful to encourage your child to follow one of the breathing exercises first, for the more relaxed they feel, the easier it will be to conjure up the images.

2) Next, ask your child to imagine they have a magic TV control in their hands. You can make this seem more real by asking them what their control looks like. What shape it is, how big it is and what you have to do to switch it on and off.

3) Then you can ask them to tell you about the scary images or nightmares they've been having. Reassure them that this technique is designed to get rid of them so they won't have to be looking at them for very long. What do the scary images look like? What's going on? What are the colours?

4) First, ask them to turn the colour down on those pictures making them less bright. They have the magic TV control in their hands and they can press a button on it to do so.

5) Next, ask if the image is moving or still. If it's moving around, get them to press 'pause'. Bring the picture to a halt – a complete standstill – a freeze.

6) Then, if they can hear any dialogue, music or sounds (roaring monsters?) along with the image, ask them to turn the volume right down. All the way down until it's silent.

7) Continue working together to adjust the picture some more if it needs it. Drain all the colour out of it, making it black and white and removing any traces of sound.

8) Next, begin shrinking it right down till it's nothing more than a dot. A tiny, tiny dot that just disappears.

9) Finally, click the 'off' button on this imaginary TV control.

After all, if you were watching something on a real TV that you weren't enjoying, you'd switch it off, wouldn't you?

You can finish by asking your child to put a good picture in place instead. What's their favourite TV show? Would they be happy with an image of a super-hero or perhaps the family pet to keep them happy? Conjure up a new image that allows them to relax and sleep looking at good pictures instead.

MINDFULNESS FOR KIDS

Children are rarely still and quiet nowadays thanks to continuous stimulation from out-of-school activities and handheld electronic devices that offer round the clock entertainment, never mind their supply of adrenalin pumping computer games. It's not surprising that it's becoming harder for children to keep a lid on their emotions and think before they act. Achieving a state of complete silence, peace and calm is way out of the reach for most children.

The Montessori Silence Game is something I used to teach the children in my school and it was astonishing to watch children, some as young as three, become enthralled with the idea of achieving a state of complete silence and stillness.

Dr Maria Montessori looked upon the creation of the Silence Game as much more than simply the absence of noise – children's imaginations benefit from having the free space and thinking time, allowing them to develop their creative talents and the relaxing effects of this exercise also reduce anxiety levels.

Learning how to take control of the body through the power of the mind is also the first step towards reducing impulsive behaviour as children develop a higher sense of awareness of what is happening around them. It is an integration of the whole being – mastery of mind over body and it strengthens the will of the children to create this state for themselves. I'd recommend you playing it with your children.

The Montessori Silence Game

1) Invite your children to play a game with you and seat them in a large circle on the floor.

2) Ensure that they are sitting in a position that's the most comfortable – not touching each other and with plenty of space between .

3) You are all going to be playing a game that consists of not moving at all! Explain that everyone is going to keep very, very quiet and very, very still. Every bit of their body needs to be still and quiet.

4) You'll be using your voice to lead the children in the direction of complete and utter stillness, so lower your voice so it sounds relaxing. Speak slowly and leave plenty of time between each instruction for those children who are slower to catch up. Towards the end you can start to whisper your instructions to highlight the fact that things are getting quieter and quieter.

Begin this process by saying:

- Let's keep our feet very still, so even our toes become still.
- Pause – wait for everyone to join in.
- Now let's keep our legs very still.
- Now our bodies very still.
- Next our arms very, very still.

- Peaceful and quiet.
- Next, our hands very still, even our fingers, very still.
- Now our heads very still.
- Our mouths and eyes very still.
- Let's close our eyes so that even our eyelids are quite, quite still.
- All peaceful and quiet.

If the earlier environment was quite noisy and exuberant, the sound of this silence and the sense of deep stillness in the air, will be really intriguing and exciting for the children.

You can say;

"Do you know what just happened?"

Then answer your own question with; *"You made a silence."*

The length of time that you play this game can be gradually extended as they become more proficient in their ability to keep totally still.

Have faith that gradually each child will join in with the game. To begin with you may find one child enjoys playing up and acting out in front of the group. Say nothing, for that would break the silence. Simply smile and allow the sound of your breathing to calm and relax the atmosphere.

Once your children are experienced at making a silence, you can progress to the next stage; listening out for sounds. Once a silence has been achieved, you can say;

"Now we can begin to listen."

After about two minutes of silence, you can go round the group one at a time and ask them what they heard during the silence game. One may have heard the sound of breathing or a clock ticking and another a bird tweeting outside or a train passing by.

If you usually play this game indoors, you can extend it by saying;

"I wonder what would happen if we played this game outside? What sounds would we hear then?" And then next time you can move outside to play it again.

WORDS THAT WORK

- *It's only natural that you feel anxious when a wasp flies near you but as each week passes, you're becoming more and more relaxed about them. Don't you think?*

- *Yes, standing on stage in front of the rest of your class can be worrying and because you are a calm person, you'll be able to handle this situation easily...*

- *So you've been feeling worried about your exams – to make yourself aware of that you need to do something more about them?*

- *Stop. That's good – now let's breathe out slowly together.*

- *I can sense that you're worried about switching the light off when you go to bed tonight BUT as you become better and better at using your 'Magic TV Control' you'll quickly see the difference it makes.*

- *Feeling anxious is quite natural and usually it encourages you to think up of ways you can do something about it.*

WORDS THAT DON'T WORK

- *Don't be so stupid! No-one else is scared of wasps...*
- *Why do you have to be such a baby?*
- *There's always something the matter with you...*
- *Pull yourself together*

- *Watch what you're doing or you'll break your neck and end up in hospital*
- *Oh, you make me feel really nervous climbing up that high slide*
- *Be careful / watch out / mind you don't hurt yourself…*

Finally, do remember it's common for worries, fears and phobias to get passed down from one generation to the next. Don't allow your own fears to make your child more fearful – they can easily be treated. You can read more about solving fears and phobias in *"Fix Your Life with NLP"* (Simon & Schuster 2012).

Other helpful resources – Relax Now, A Magic Day Out
Boost Your Confidence available from www.success-4-kids.com

5

Boosting Confidence

Does your child sing like an X Factor winner in the privacy of the bathroom, only to shrivel with embarrassment when performing in front of others? Do you long to have their talents recognised outside the home? Does the idea of music exams make your child feel like quitting an instrument before they've even got properly started?

We all want confident kids. In fact, it's the number one request from parents who come to see me at my practice.

It might help initially to pause for a moment and ask ourselves what exactly confidence is. How does it differ from self-esteem and how do we know when we've got it?

We've all seen children who strut around the playground constantly bragging and boasting. A bit too boisterous and loud, they're invariably pushing to be first in the queue. Few of us would want our children to behave like that because it's pretty obvious that overly confident 'outside' behaviour doesn't really match a person's 'inside' feelings. It's simply there to mask feelings of insecurity and they're not genuinely confident children.

Confidence is having the belief that you can succeed at something. It's possible to be confident about one area of your life but totally unconfident about another. 'I'm confident that I can bake a cake but I'm not at all confident about playing the piano in the school concert.'

Your self-esteem on the other hand, is related to a broad sense of personal value or self-worth. It's not a quality that changes very much as it's more about how you see yourself as a person in general, rather than your ability to specifically do something. Discussing your family's values (with regards to honesty, trust, work, spirituality etc.) will encourage this part of your child's identity to develop more easily. They'll get a sense of who and what they are from your family's 'brand'.

Building confidence comes from taking action and trying out things that are difficult – stepping out of the comfort zone. It's not about being perfect, it's about facing obstacles and realising that it's ok to fail – you can always have another go.

In the early years, confidence develops from becoming successful at doing things independently round the home – the more opportunities you can put in your child's path, the better. For example, a low-level bathroom mirror on the wall for brushing teeth and child-height hooks in the cupboard for coats.

Patience from you, also plays a part. If you cannot wait patiently for your child to do up their shoelaces, climb a flight of stairs or cut up their own food, you'll be denting their confidence. Diving in and taking over to speed things up or showing signs of frustration will not foster feelings of success.

Likewise telling your child that they're not reciting their poem well enough and should put more effort into it, will not enable them to stand on stage and give an Oscar winning performance. Using negative phrases such as *"Don't speak so quietly – no-one will hear you"* will ensure that you get just that: a quiet child that no-one can hear.

DEVELOPING RESILIENCE

In today's society there are more and more ways in which we hold a 'mirror' up to our children, pointing out their shortcomings and inadequacies. Thanks to the new 'selfie culture' it's not easy to hide that zit on the end of your nose, or your lank, greasy hair. And it's the same at school. Perpetual SATS tests and examinations mean that today's children are 'weighed, measured and tested' more than any other generation and from a far earlier age too. No wonder it results in anxious, worried children who lack the confidence to step outside into the big, wide world.

It's often been said that life is a contact sport, so it's inevitable that sooner or later, we're going to get hurt. Boosting your child's 'resilience' is what will inoculate them against life's knocks and setbacks. It gives them the ability to pick themselves up, dust themselves down and carry on.

Resilient children:

- Have the ability to bounce back from negative situations.
- Tend to be more optimistic in their outlook.

- Can think creatively when faced with difficulties.
- Are socially competent with close friendships.
- Are able to communicate well.

Resilience is a skill that anyone can learn and given that your child is unlikely to pass every exam they sit, sail through every job interview they attend and find that the path of true love runs smoothly, it's a valuable resource to have.

As a key member of your child's 'support team' you can:

1) Help them to see negative events as part and parcel of day-to-day life. It's not an automatic disaster if something goes wrong; it just means that a different solution needs to be found. Talk openly about mistakes that you may have made yourself and laugh about them: *"Silly me, I put my car keys in the fridge!"* or *"That recipe didn't work well did it? I thought it tasted odd. Next time, I'll try it without the tomatoes and I'll add carrots instead."* Don't pretend everything is always perfect.

2) If your child seems to be repeatedly failing, check that they're not setting unrealistic goals for themselves. Help your child to break goals down into smaller steps, so that they become more manageable.

3) Teach your child to problem-solve by bouncing ideas around at a Family Conference. Not every idea that gets mentioned will be a good one, but this is a natural part of the process. Write them down and tell your child that the aim is to come up with 10 different solutions to each problem, however wacky they may seem and then you can reject the ones you decide not to use.

4) Get more involved with school life, whether it's as a parent doing things like baking cakes for the school fete or building scenery for the end of term play, or encouraging your child to join the choir or sports team. Attending all the events that happen out of school hours as a family, will help your child feel that this is somewhere he truly belongs.

5) Most importantly – model the behaviour you wish to see. Demonstrate good communication skills in your own relationships and start incorporating these 'bounce-back' skills in your own attitude to daily life.

DEALING WITH NEGATIVE THINKING

Negative thinking is a bad habit that many children (and adults for that matter) slip into. Left unchecked, it begins to eat away at confidence levels, so watch out for the language that your child is using and reframe their sentences with a positive spin.

For example, if your child says:

"There won't be anyone at my new school who likes me."

It may seem tempting to reply with:
"Don't be so daft, of course there will."

But it's better to give a fuller, more considered answer with a positive outlook.

"I completely understand why you're worried that you won't make any new friends, but the advantage of going to a bigger school is that there will be many more children to choose from than there ever were at your junior school. So, the chances of meeting new friends you will get along with are actually very high. Yes, I dare say you'll come across one or two children who you won't like and likewise, perhaps they won't be keen on being friendly with you either, but you can simply see that as an opportunity to move on and get to know other new people."

OR

"Do we have to go to Grandma's house? It's so boring there!"

Rather than replying:

"Yes you do. Stop moaning because you'll be fine when you get there."

It would be better to reframe your answer as:

"I know it's not the same as being at home with your computer games, nor will you have your friends there, but remember how much you enjoyed going last time. When you walked her dog Rolo down by the riverbank, he jumped in and chased those swans and made us all laugh. I wonder what he'll get up to this time."

Negative thinking, along with whingeing, whining and moaning can easily become a habit that's hard to break. Switching your child's thought patterns around will help to prevent this from happening. And don't forget to keep a check on yourself too. Is your own negative outlook fuelling your child's negativity perhaps?

Use this **POSITIVE THINKING** exercise:

This activity is ideal for children (and adults) who generally feel quite negative about their lives and struggle to see the good side. Talking about positive events will start to release serotonin and gradually begin to alter brain chemistry. Keep this up for at least one month and ideally allow it to become a natural part of your family life.

1) Encourage your child to start keeping a journal or diary. They can use a physical notebook to record events or doodle in, or they can use their smart phones or tablet device for the same purpose. They can call their journal anything they like: Happiness Diary, Sunshine book… etc.

2) Ask your child to write down three positive things that happened in their day. These can be quite simple things to begin with eg: We had pizza for lunch and it's my favourite; the maths teacher forgot to set homework for us; it was a sunny day today and we played outside.

3) Repeat this on a daily basis.

If your child is reluctant to physically sit down and do this on a daily basis, introduce this technique conversationally, either in the car on the way home from school, or as you're sitting round the dinner table, or in the evenings at bath-time. You can start the ball rolling by mentioning something really good that happened to yourself during the day – and then taking turns.

If your child really cannot come up with three positive things that happened in their day, then my recommendation is to increase the required number to five or even ten things. Strange as it may seem, this will help to free up your child's mind and they'll start to notice smaller, less significant occurrences eg. a butterfly flew into the room; I watched one of my favourite TV programmes.

Bear in mind, it's the flow of the thought patterns that's the important bit and not the events themselves. Once you've got this going in the right direction, you'll quickly see how it becomes a natural part of your child's thinking.

EMBARRASSMENT AND BLUSHING

We've all experienced those moments of self-consciousness that irritatingly trigger off a reddening of the skin – most usually on the face. Blushing from embarrassment is connected to your 'fight-or-flight' response. As you find yourself in an awkward situation, your body automatically releases a rush of adrenaline that then causes your breathing and heart rate to speed up, enabling you to run away from this perceived danger, if you need to.

Adrenaline also causes your blood vessels to dilate in order to improve blood flow and oxygen delivery and this is the case with blushing. The veins in your face dilate and as more blood flows through them, your face becomes red. If your child suffers from this problem, then reducing their overall anxiety levels would help to keep a control over the amount of adrenaline being produced. You can read more about how to do this in Chapter Four, Eliminating Fears and Anxiety.

Client Case Study: Rebecca aged 17 years

Here's how I worked with a young client who came to see me for help with dealing with this problem. Rebecca was leaving school and about to attend a job interview. Her biggest worry was that she wouldn't be able to speak confidently and that she'd start blushing as soon as she opened her mouth. Notice how powerful words really can be:

When Rebecca came to see me I asked her to think back to the last time she blushed. Could she remember what she was saying to herself? Usually people's internal dialogue goes something along the lines of:

"Oh no, I think I'm going to go red. Yes, I am, I just know it – I'm turning red. I hope they don't notice my face going red. I can feel it – it's starting to turn red. Great, last thing I wanted – my face going red!"

She agreed and realised exactly why her face did turn red. Her internal dialogue issued a command, her mind created a picture and her body followed – doing exactly as she had told it to.

I explained that she could easily take control of this by giving a different sort of command. The next time she felt herself starting to get that rush of adrenaline that signalled that her face might start turning red, all she simply needed to say was:

"I think I'm turning BLUE – yes, I am – I'm turning BLUE. I can feel that BLUENESS start to spread now across my face, my chest and down my arms even – I'm turning BLUE."

As it's usual to feel heat rising up our faces, instruct this feeling to travel in a downwards direction, like so:

"I can feel the BLUE start to drain down from the top of my head, down through my face, my eyes, my cheeks . . . down my neck, my shoulders, my chest. Yes, I'm definitely turning BLUE."

And you can also add other suggestions such as a bucket of ice being tipped over the head or just a couple of ice cubes sitting on top of the head.

You can test this out – it works!

AN EXTRA BOOST OF CONFIDENCE

If your child needs an extra boost of confidence for a future event such as a party, an exam, an audition, stage performance, job interview or sporting event, there is an NLP technique that will also really help. You can do this indoors or outdoors in the garden or park, whichever feels most comfortable for your child.

CIRCLE OF CONFIDENCE

1. Create a circle on the floor or ground using: a piece of chalk; a long piece of cord, ribbon or string; or a plastic hula-hoop.

2. Whilst standing outside the circle, ask your child to think about the challenging situation that's coming up in the future and discuss it. Ask them to take a few moments to consider it. Who will be there? Where it will be? How much time will there be? What is the desired outcome?

3. Encourage them to think about the resources or skills they'll

need. For example, an audition or stage performance requires a bit of star quality; a job interview requires you to be confident and able to think freely; an exam or sports event may require you to be calm and focused.

4. Position your child so they're standing with a good, confident posture or pose. A super-hero pose with legs apart and hands on hips is good for this. Ask them to have a good picture in their mind of how they'd like the event to go. They can describe it to you, with prompts if needed.

5. Now, ask them to recall a time in the past when they had all of the resources that they'll need at this upcoming event. So even if the stage performance is their first one, perhaps they sang a song loudly or danced enthusiastically during a game at a friend's birthday party. Likewise for a job interview, you could encourage them to recall a time in the past when they confidently explained to a relative or family friend what they'd like to do when they leave school. For an exam, remember a time in the past when an exam or class test did go well.

6. When all the resources that will be needed have been remembered, ask your child to step into the magic circle, close their eyes and relive that time again. Talk it through with them, encouraging them to see what they saw, hear what they heard, feel what they felt and make that image in their mind grow and grow. As the picture grows so too will the strength of their feelings. You can embellish this image, by asking them to turn the colours up more brightly and the sounds more loudly – a bit like having their own personal TV control.

7. Ask them to squeeze together either their fist (for younger children) or their thumb and middle finger on the dominant hand (better for older children and teens) to 'capture' all of those good feelings. Do this for at least 30 seconds. This is known as 'anchoring' – attaching all the good feelings to a trigger.

8. Next, they can relax the hand and step out of the circle.

9. Then, ask them to think of another feeling or resource they'll need to handle this future situation well. Search back through the memories once more to remember a time in the past when they had exactly that resource.

10. Ask your child to step back into the circle again and run through Steps 6 and 7 once more, with this new memory.

11. Once finished, let them step back out of your circle.

12. Tell your child to relax and now, and suggest they think of a friend real or imagined) they'd like to have alongside them as a support at this future event. It could even be the family pet or a favourite TV character.

13. Get them to hop back into the circle and run through Steps 6 and 7 once more with all the good feelings that having this imaginary buddy alongside them gives them.

14. Let them come back out of the circle.

15. Once you have gathered together and anchored all the resources and feelings your child will need or want for this event, get them to jump back into your circle once more.

16. Now, with eyes closed, ask them to visualise that future event going just the way they'd like it to. Describe the event from start to finish for them as they imagine it in their minds. As you do this, ask them to squeeze their fist (if they used it first time around) or thumb and middle finger and automatically those good, good feelings will flood their body as they mentally rehearse the upcoming challenging situation. Fill in the details so they can see what they'll be wearing; see the other people there; notice their posture, composure, tone of voice, feelings of inner strength – not forgetting, of course,

the relaxed smile on their face – the sign that tells them all is going well.

17. They can imagine the circle has a colour – a good strong colour – one that represents confidence and success to them.

18. As they stand in the circle with eyes closed, ask them to imagine this colour rising up in a mist all around them. As it travels up, they can imagine it swirling around all the way to the top of their head and beyond.

19. Why not add a bit of stardust to it for good measure?

20. Congratulations – you've just set up a Confidence Anchor for your child. They can open their eyes, relax their hand and step out of the circle.

Encourage your child to practice this again – the more it gets practiced, the stronger the feelings of confidence will be. Then when they experience the future event for real, they can either squeeze that fist or thumb and middle finger together again, and all these resourceful feelings will flood their body once more. This will enable them to handle the situation in just the way they want – with extra confidence!

THE POWER OF BELIEF

"Whether you believe you can, or believe you can't – you're probably right."

Henry Ford

Our beliefs are a very powerful force and influence everything we do. Put simply, if you cannot 'see' yourself being successful then your chances of succeeding will be very slim.

One of my favourite stories that demonstrates the power of our beliefs is the story of Roger Bannister, the first person to run a mile in under four minutes, back in 1954. For many years, runners had dreamed of breaking the record but none had been successful. Indeed, doctors had declared it an impossibility, fearing the heart would spontaneously combust under the pressure. Bannister, however, was determined and against advice organised a race that saw him not only achieve his goal of four minutes, but beat it with seconds to spare. News of his achievement spread around the world.

Interestingly, whilst no one in the history of running had been able to achieve that record-breaking time, as soon as Bannister did it, other athletes went on to do the same over the course of the next two years.

It would not have been surprising if one or two more had achieved the same time, but the fact that a whole cluster of runners went on to also do it, demonstrates that as soon as they had the concrete evidence that it really was possible, their performance automatically matched their altered beliefs.

I told this story to my son when he was 13 years old and suffering from a last minute bout of school Sports Day nerves. Tom was and still is, passionate about sport and very good at it. He was on target to do very well in his events but started to doubt his abilities. I talked to him about how seeing himself as a winner would alter his performance enough to create a 'difference that would make all the difference.'

I asked him to close his eyes and we ran through the Circle of Confidence exercise and set up an 'anchor' for him. Later as he was tucked up in bed and going off to sleep, I described a movie called 'Tom's Perfect Sports Day'. I encouraged him to see himself winning and being successful – and I left him with these thoughts drifting round inside his mind.

The next day – well, what can I say? Tom won each of his three events, plus the Field Events Cup, the Senior Cup and overall Victor's Cup – coming home with six cups and medals to match. Reader – let me tell you, of course we were both delighted but at the same time just a little bit embarrassed. Word spread that I had 'hypnotised' my child the night before and the Headmaster's wife started to question whether this should be considered as cheating.

When all the fuss had died down, it did make me stop and wonder what greatness any of our kids could achieve with that extra ounce of confidence and the belief that winning really is possible.

WORDS THAT WORK

- *I love being with you and us spending time together*
- *I felt so proud of you…*
- *I really care about you*
- *You're such fun to be with*
- *You're a really good friend – it's good to see take care of others*
- *Look at you – all smartly dressed – you have good eye for colour*
- *I really value your opinion*
- *What do you think?*
- *I trust you*
- *I have every faith in you*
- *Not so long ago, you were struggling… and you can do this easily*
- *You've come a long way*
- *Learning new things every day*

WORDS THAT DON'T WORK

- *Your sister can do it, so why can't you?*
- *What's the matter with you? Pull yourself together*
- *You'll be fine when you get there*
- *You're always so clumsy / careless / stupid / silly*
- *Don't be so daft*
- *Hurry up – I haven't got all day, you know*
- *You're always moaning..*
- *Trust you to be the trouble-maker*
- *I can't leave you alone for five minutes, can I?*
- *You're the quiet one / the shy one*
- *Don't speak so quietly, no-one will hear you.*

Other helpful resources – Relax Now, A Magic Day Out, Boost Your Confidence CD/MP3s available from www.success-4-kids.com

6

Changing Unwanted Habits and Behaviours

Oh, those irritating habits! There can't be a parent in the land who hasn't experienced the frustration that comes with all that thumb-sucking, nail-biting, hair-pulling or more ongoing problems such as bedwetting, facial tics, nervous coughs and stammers. And the ridiculous thing is that the more you tell your child to stop, the more they seem to do it! Stuck with this never-ending cycle of unwanted behaviour, you can't see a way out of it for your child.

Well, let me start by explaining about how habits are made and how they can be broken.

MAKING A HABIT

Each time any of us undertakes a brand new activity such as riding a bicycle, tying a shoelace, learning to drive a car, or dance a tango, a new neural pathway is created in our brain. Each time we repeat this new activity or pattern of behaviour, it's like a crackle of electricity travelling down this pathway over and over again. With time, the more we repeat the activity, the more the neural pathway becomes established. This new behaviour then becomes part of what we call our 'subconscious' mind.

You may remember me explaining this in Chapter One. The subconscious mind is the reason why you find that you no longer have to think 'consciously' about how to drive a car, as you did when you were learning to drive and taking all those lessons. With your subconscious mind acting as your 'auto-pilot', you can drive a car without thinking about it at all.

The subconscious mind is a very clever system that we're all born with. It gives us the ability to download, if you like, all our habits and behaviours. It speeds things up for us so we don't have to learn how to drive a car all over again each time we sit in it and means we can do more than one thing at a time.

So far, so good.

The downside, as most of us have already discovered, is the subconscious mind isn't all that picky or choosy. It will download and store ALL your habits and patterns of behaviours. That's great if it's a good pattern and something we want to keep on doing, but not so good if it's a bad habit that we'd rather be without, such as biting our fingernails or eating too many chocolate bars.

Those bad habits become deeply embedded in our subconscious mind and when we try to stop doing them, we find it hard to do. We feel 'odd' without them and our mind will drag us back into that familiar pattern of behaviour, simply because it feels more comfortable to do so. It thinks it's doing the right thing for us.

The problems start when we try to unpick or erase these habits that have almost been 'tattooed' on our minds. Our conscious mind might be thinking that now would be a good time to go on a diet, but our subconscious mind will be telling us that we need to eat chocolate every day because that's what we've always done.

A struggle starts between these two parts – and that's why willpower on it's own often fails.

The good news is, not all is lost. If we can stop doing the activity, or behaving in a particular way, the neural pathway will gradually shrink and eventually disappear completely.

This is why you'll find a 21 day Success Journal at the back of this book. I want to help you create a new habit, a new way of thinking about your parenting so you can easily start to implement changes to your language patterns. You see, I know it's going to be more effective if you can practice a little bit each day. The success journal will help to keep you on track.

Taking repetitive action in the right way will help this new way of thinking feel completely natural and normal to you. Pretty soon you'll be able to use 'the language of persuasion' with your kids, without even realising that you're doing it.

For now though, let's focus on some of your children's bad habits and I'll list some useful tips to make it easier for you to help them change. I'm going to focus on just a couple of bad habits here but the principles for changing any kind of behaviour patterns are going to be the same, so you can adapt them to suit your child's particular problem.

THUMB-SUCKING AND NAIL-BITING

Thumb-sucking and nail-biting are common enough activities amongst young children who naturally find it comforting. We're all born with a strong sucking instinct and a desire to explore things with our mouths – our survival depends on it.

Most children will go on to outgrow these annoying habits in middle childhood without too much cajoling. For others, change will come when external events such as a trip to the dentist for corrective braces, presents them with no option but something such as nail-biting, can continue for a lifetime.

Repeated reminders to stop rarely work and it can become stressful for both parent and child. Once bad feelings become associated with the habit, anxiety takes hold fuelling the child's desire for more comfort. It's a catch-22 situation.

Identify connecting habits: Our habits connect with other habits and form a kind of 'network' or spider's web in our minds. For example, if your child starts to chew their fingernails or suck their thumb each time they're sitting in the back of the car, a connection will be made between these two activities and this can become a powerful force. No matter how badly your child wants to grow long fingernails in the future, they'll find that long car journeys prove to be a struggle. Breaking this link could be as simple as switching the side of the car that they usually sit on. If they're used to sucking their thumb and leaning on the window for example, it won't feel quite the same if they sit on the other side. The brain will become confused and you'll have a 'window of opportunity' to break the habit.

Substitution: Sometimes, I do encourage parents to consider introducing an alternative or substitute behaviour to their child. Take some time to notice the comfort that they're getting from the habit and suggest a suitable substitute. Choose your substitution carefully though, for it won't do to acquire a new habit that you'll want your child to unhook themselves from later eg. chewing sweets. The new piece of behaviour could be as simple as a 'doing' activity, such as applying moisturizer to the fingertips, or 'not doing' such as tucking hands under the legs so they can 'rest and relax' here, or keeping the thumb 'dry'. Be sure to decide what it's going to be well in advance, because it will make committing to it easier. Discuss this with your child and allow them to come up with ideas that appeal to them.

Always say what you DO want: We learnt all about the destructive powers of telling your child what NOT to do in the Words that Work section. Remember your words are creating pictures in the mind and your child will be magnetically drawn to these. Avoid telling them to 'stop' doing something.

Avoid rewards: Studies show that rewards such as money, sweets, trainers or the promise of trips to the theme park can actually hamper your child's efforts to be successful. Not only does this take the child's attention, awareness and focus off the task in hand, but once the reward has been received, the temptation to go back to the old habit will be high, simply because there's no enticement any longer. Perhaps you know someone who's been offered money to quit smoking. They can grit their teeth and keep it up for long enough to receive payment but once that part of the bargain is over, they quickly revert back to the cigarettes. It will always be easier to break a habit when the 'reward' is the benefit that comes as a result of stopping the negative behaviour eg: nice long fingernails, straight teeth, dry beds leading to sleepovers with friends. You can read more about rewards in your Parenting Toolkit in Chapter 11.

Speed up gratification: Many of us struggle with the notion of 'delayed gratification' – we want results fast and we want them now. Speed up the good feelings your child will get once they've rid themselves of this bad habit, by encouraging them to sit, dream and imagine a time in the future when all is well. Allow them to create an image of a bright, new shiny future for themselves when the habit has been well and truly dispensed with. This only needs to take a few minutes and you can tell them that they're using exactly the same techniques that top athletes and sports people use to perfect their performance. The more we can see ourselves behaving in a certain way, the more likely we are to get there.

Reverse Psychology: It's possible to create confusion in a thumb-sucking child's mind by encouraging them to suck more, not less. Children are used to being told that it's good to share and to take turns, so telling them that it's only fair that the other thumb and fingers all have a turn too can be enough to break the cycle. Each day, it will be a different finger or thumb's turn to be sucked and it will mean that they have to go 10 days without sucking their favourite one. You can also use phrases such as *"I'm not going to tell you to stop sucking your thumb because I know that you'll know which time will be just right for you. In fact, you've probably already started to notice this, haven't you?"* Don't expect an answer – simply leave the phrase hanging there.

Keep a Photo Diary: Being able to see that we're making progress, however small the steps, is what keeps us motivated and on track. With cameras built into mobile phones nowadays, it's going to be easy to keep a photo diary. Encourage your child to take a photo of their fingernails (or thumb) each day and notice the changes. After a couple of weeks, they can compare and contrast, or even put the footage together to create a short video, watching their very own fingernails grow.

Create a 'Disaster Movie': I would only recommend this exercise for an older child that is desperate to stop biting their nails say, or pulling out their hair and gives you their consent to do this. Perhaps they've had many failed attempts at breaking their unwanted habit and are willing to give anything a go. None of us really knows what we look like when we 'do' our bad habit and if anyone tells us we look daft or unappealing, we simply feel cross rather than motivated to stop. However, you can take a few candid videos of your child chewing their nails (preferably using their phone) and couple this with photographs of sore and bleeding fingers too. They can watch these as they make a list of 10 reasons why they're really keen to ditch this miserable habit. Remind them that the habit may feel comforting whilst they're doing it but the reality is what they're seeing in the pictures. The more they do this, the more motivated and committed they'll become.

BEDWETTING

Nearly a million children in the UK and around five million in the US, continue to accidentally wet their beds at night after the age of six years. So if your child is one of these, they're in good company. It's also affecting older children and teenagers more than ever before, with supermarkets routinely stocking night time nappies for 9-15 year olds. Once the habit becomes deeply ingrained in the subconscious mind, it can become hard to stop.

Bedwetting was once considered to be the result of anxiety-related problems and something to be ashamed of, meaning that it was rarely discussed openly. Fortunately, attitudes are changing now with more thought being given to the possible causes.

Experts are beginning to agree that factors in our modern-day Western lifestyle are more likely to be the cause. Some of the reasons given for this increasing problem are:

- The superior absorbency of modern-day nappies that prevent children from feeling wet and learning how to stay dry.
- Busy family lives that interfere with consistent training methods if child-minding is frequently shared.
- The poor quality of school toilets and lack of opportunities to drink water throughout the day.
- Our highly processed Western diet that causes constipation.

Traditional solutions to the problem are limited but the first step should always be a check up with your child's doctor to rule out any underlying urine infections. What often happens to the many children who struggle to get dry after the age of eight or so, is a referral to a specialist Enuresis Clinic where doctors can prescribe medications that help to dry up bodily fluids and reduce the quantity of urine produced. In some cases, anti-depressants are also prescribed.

Other options are alarms that buzz or ring when dampness is felt, but often these are less popular with children and so their use is quickly discontinued.

Frustrated with the lack of options available to children who find themselves stuck with this miserable problem, I developed my 'Stop Bedwetting in 7 Days' programme available both in book and video formats[2].

To summarise, bedwetting is unlike other habits such as thumb sucking, nail-biting and hair-pulling, where the child needs to 'stop' doing something to enable the established neural pathway to shrink and eventually disappear. With bedwetting we're asking the child to not only 'stop' wetting the bed at night thereby breaking the link in that pathway, but to also 'start' a new habit and develop a brand new

[2]   Stop Bedwetting in Seven Days – www.stopbedwettingin7days.co.uk

neural pathway. This new pathway will create better communication between the bladder and the brain, sending signals and messages more effectively. Only when the child starts to receive these messages can he begin to deal with the problem, either by waking up at night to visit the bathroom, or to hold on and wait till morning.

IT'S GOOD TO TALK

It's only natural that many families avoid talking about their child's bedwetting habit. We often hear that it's best not to make 'an issue' out of it and that it will somehow go away by itself. But for all too many children this simply doesn't happen. And as the child gets older, the situation becomes increasingly stressful and embarrassing, meaning there's even less conversation about it.

I would encourage every parent to read up as much as possible about the problem and then decide to have a proper conversation. Here's what happened to one of my clients:

Elizabeth called me to arrange an appointment for her daughter. Eight year old Sophie was still wearing pull-ups at night and there did not seem to be an end in sight. Elizabeth had avoided discussing the problem as she hadn't wanted to embarrass her daughter and make an issue out of it. Doctors had reassured her that Sophie would simply 'grow out it'. But now, a school trip was looming and her daughter was going to stay away from home for two nights. She needed to be dry at night for this.

Having got a date in the diary to see me, Elizabeth sat down and told Sophie all about it. To her astonishment, Sophie was relieved to hear that she wouldn't need to wear a pull-up or night-time nappy any more.

You see, kids aren't mind-readers and sometimes they just don't know what we want them to do. In the case of my client, her daughter thought she wasn't allowed to get up out of bed at night to visit the bathroom, because her mum gave her a pull-up to wear every night.

'Why didn't you say something sooner?' she asked her mum. 'I can easily get up and use the bathroom all by myself. I've been waiting for you to stop giving me those pull-ups to wear.'

Problem solved!

Visualisation exercises can be very useful: quite simply, this is where you see yourself behaving in the new, more desired manner and this encourages the new neural pathway to develop much more rapidly. It speeds the whole process up. As I said, top athletes and sports people know that the secret to success is taking control of their bodies through the power of the mind. For me, it made perfect sense to follow the same process to help children overcome the bedwetting habit.

Here's an extract from my best-selling **"Stop Bedwetting in 7 Days Programme"** so you can see the type of exercises that are included:

Exercise – 1st Stage – Water Balloon Experiment

The aim of this exercise is to teach your child about the muscles around the bladder that tighten and then relax and release, as and when we need them to, simply by thinking about the process. Our thoughts control this mechanical opening and closing of the bladder.

You may find it easier to do this exercise in the bath, rather than at the kitchen sink!

1. Take an ordinary party balloon (a round one is best) and attach it to the end of a cold water tap.

2. Switch the tap on slowly and watch as the water begins to fill the balloon. Keep going until it's a bit bigger than a tennis ball. Switch the water off. Now, very carefully take the balloon off the tap and squeeze the open end between your thumb and one of your fingers, to make sure the water can't come out.

3. Turn the balloon upside down over the sink. This is similar to how your bladder looks. Slowly, begin to relax your fingers slightly and allow some water to begin trickling out of the end. This is just how water comes out of your bladder when you go to the toilet.

4. Now let's see if we can stop this flow. Squeeze your fingers tight once more and you'll discover that you can easily stop the water coming out.

5. And loosen your grip and relax once more.

6. And then squeeze them tightly shut to stop the flow once more.

This is exactly how your muscles work – squeezing tight to hold urine in the bladder and relaxing to let it out – just like opening and closing a gate.

You can practise this exercise again, if you want to. Keeping this gate tightly closed is just what your body needs to learn to do at night to help you keep your bed dry.

Exercise – 2nd Stage – Creating A 'Gate' For The Bladder

Now that your child has got the idea of how the muscles open and close – just like a gate or door – around the opening of the bladder, you can encourage them to create one in their mind's eye.

1. Settle yourselves down somewhere comfortable. Ask your child to close his eyes and just take a few moments to visualise the gate to his bladder. Pause for a few moments to give your child time to do this.

2. Encourage him to describe it clearly to you:

- what colour is it?
- how does it open?
- does it have a lock or bolt on it?
- is the lock tightly shut right now?

3. Ask your child to explain what needs to be done to make sure this gate is firmly shut at night. Do check that your child's gate will stem the flow of urine well enough. Some children design gates that have holes or gaps in them. Use the word 'door' instead if you feel this would be more suitable. Allow your child's imagination to take over here – some children invent 'gatekeepers' to stand guard at night using their favourite superhero or even family pet. Others put extra big locks on the gate.

4. Finally, ask your child to draw a picture of this special gate or door. When all the details have been filled in, they can stick this up on their bedroom wall by the side of the bed. Each night before they go to sleep, they can simply look at this picture as a reminder and 'lock their gate' so no leaks occur at night time.

Reminder: it's good to repeat this exercise along with filling up the balloon several times throughout the week.

As simple as this all sounds, I already know that there are some children out there who will become dry at night, simply by following these two steps. Visualisation techniques are truly wonderful and never cease to amaze me.

You can read more about the full programme here:
www.stopbedwettingin7days.co.uk

WORDS THAT WORK

- *When you stop...* (presupposition that problem will be overcome)
- *Just imagine how good it will feel to...*
- *I noticed that you're finding it easier to keep your nails looking nice*
- *I can see that you're keeping your thumb dry*
- *How would you feel if you could successfully overcome this problem?*
- *I expect you're already starting to wonder how good it's going to feel when...*

You may also like to introduce a little reverse psychology:

- *It's not as if I'm suggesting that you give up sucking your thumb right now*
- *There's no need to do this right now*
- *I'm not suggesting that you'll immediately begin to see the benefits of...*
- *It's good to share – so do make sure all your fingers get a turn*

WORDS THAT DON'T WORK

- *Don't do that*
- *How many times have I told you not to...*
- *Can't you just stop...*
- *If you don't stop chewing your finger nails, your teeth will fall out*
- *You'll end up with a deformed thumb*
- *No-one will ever find you attractive*
- *Everyone will laugh at you*
- *Think of the embarrassment*

None of these statements will put your child in a confident, resourceful state where they feel able to get to grips with ditching their bad habit. Chipping away at their self-confidence will not help.

7

Homework and Exam Stress

Children as young as four years old are now routinely given, at the very least, reading homework to complete on a nightly basis. Schools recommend youngsters continue work throughout the holiday periods too. It all adds up to a lot of pressure both on parents and children. Parents don't want their child to lag behind his peers and the more they worry about this, the more anxious the child becomes. It is a recipe for homework disaster. Parents demand their children start studying, children push back and the arguments begin. The ludicrous scenario ensues that in the amount of time a homework argument takes, the child could have done the assignment three times over!

So, how do you put an end to homework battles?

Develop a regular routine for your child. Work out the best time of day and also the best place for it. Some children are unable to focus until they've had something to eat and drink and a bit of time to unwind. For others, it's best if they knuckle straight down the moment they get home from school and chill later. By definition, a routine is something that is done routinely – it needs to be pretty much the same every day. And every week thereafter.

Be consistent. Children who don't have anywhere in particular for homework and end up doing it on the kitchen table one night, then on the floor in front of the TV the next and maybe up in the bedroom the night after that, will not do as well as those who have a dedicated space. Likewise, children doing it before the evening meal one night and after it the next, will find it harder to make doing homework seem like a natural, automatic part of their day. Once it's imprinted on their minds as part of their daily habits and routine, you'll find there'll be less resistance.

Eliminate distractions such as pets, TV, phones and siblings. Don't be afraid to put rules in place, such as mp3 players, tablet devices and mobile phones to be kept away from the homework desk. A child that constantly jumps up and keeps running back to check his phone, is not simply being 'naughty'. He's struggling to carry out his homework and needs some extra help here. Rather than punishing him for the unwanted behaviour, take a closer look at what's preventing him from doing what he should be doing.

Don't overlook the fact that your child might be:

- Hungry
- Thirsty
- Hot
- Cold
- Or need some time to re-connect with you, his siblings or family pet after a busy day at school.

Address these needs first and you'll find homework sessions will run more smoothly.

What kind of learner is your child?

We use all our senses to absorb information from our environment and our senses form the basis of our learning preference or style. Taking a few moments to observe your child to figure which methods suit him best, may help avoid a whole lot of homework angst.

Your child may favour any of the following learning styles:

Visual. These children prefer to learn by seeing information. They like reading, pictures or diagrams, demonstrations and watching videos. Eventually they'll picture the information in their minds.

Auditory. Here they prefer to learn by hearing or saying it. They enjoy listening to CDs, lectures, debates, discussions and verbal instructions. They may ask you to repeat a set of instructions over and over again: they like hearing it being said.

Kinesthetic. Children with this preference learn best by getting a feel for it. They enjoy physical involvement, hands-on work, moving around and touching.

Lynn O'Brien of Specific Diagnostic Studies Inc, found that about 40% of people have a preference for a visual learning style, 15 percent for auditory and 45% for kinaesthetic.[3]

If you can determine your child's preferred learning style you may be able to adapt any homework activity to suit. By being creative, most tasks can be presented and carried out in a variety of ways.

For example:

For visual learners:

Create Flashcards: (You can buy ready made Flashcards, but your child will be missing out on another learning opportunity. It's best to make your own.)

1. Take a sheet of paper and draw a line down the middle.

2. In the left hand column write questions and sums that you've picked out of your child's work. Even a history essay can be broken down into questions.

---

3   Learning through the Arts, New Horizons for Learning, Seattle, 2002

3. In the right hand column write the corresponding answers. (Ask your child to do this if he's old enough to do so. Writing out the information is another form of learning.)

4. Take a photocopy of this sheet if you can.

5. Using scissors – cut down the middle and then cut between each question and answer.

6. Separate out the questions from the answers – lay out all the questions on one side of the table and all the answers on the other. Jumble them up.

7. Play the game – match the pieces of paper together so the answers go with the correct question.

8. Check your answers against the photocopy you took at the start of the game.

9. Repeat this process as many times as you need to, until all the questions and their answers are correctly matched.

Alternatively, colour code and chunk down: To learn any subject, especially say, French oral where you'll need to recite a chunk of information, write on a large white board or sheet of paper and make each paragraph a different colour. Chunk the information down. Tonight's homework is to learn the red paragraph. Tomorrow you can learn the green one.

For more kinesthetic learners:

Repeat the Flashcard game thus:

1. Place the pieces of paper on the floor – questions in one corner of the room and the answers in another. (For a really restless child, play this game "at a distance" – place one set of cards on the floor in one room and place the other set in a different room.)

2. Your child will have to run between the two rooms to match the answers to the questions.

3. Lay the pieces of paper or card out on the floor as a pair. Then check the answers are all correct by looking at your photocopy master.

4. Repeat as many times as is needed to get the answers right.

5. Now reverse the entire game, by picking up an answer and find the corresponding question.

For auditory learners:

Turn the homework into a rhyme, record it and play it back. Sing times tables in the car.

Personally I find these methods so much more appealing. Why would anyone want to sit at a desk to do this?

TIP: If your child struggles to sit still and look down at his work, buy a few rolls of plain lining wallpaper and stick large pieces of it to the bedroom wall with some tape or pins.

Now you have a blank canvas and using some pencils or felt-tipped pens, (taking care to make sure the pens do not mark the wall behind it!) your child can test his ideas out and see if the answer comes more easily.

Don't be surprised if he needs to stand back on the other side of the room to think about things before writing anything down.

This is an ideal activity for children who fidget a lot – big brushstrokes and lots of movement will suit them better. Once they've figured out their answers, they'll be happy to sit back down at their desk and 'copy' the answers across.

CAN YOUR CHILD SEE?

In Section One, I talked about how our minds automatically make pictures or images as we think or speak.

Take a few moments to think about the front door to your home.

- What colour is it?
- On which side do you put your key in the lock – the left hand side, or the right hand side?
- And whereabouts is your letter box?
- Is it horizontal or vertical?

As you were taking a few moments to consider your answers to these questions, your mind was creating images for you. Of course, they're not like photographs – they're hazy and could be black and white or colour – but nevertheless, they're there and are very important.

As your child sits and thinks about his schoolwork, he'll be doing the same; looking out in front of him to 'see' the image that's being created. It's how artists decide on a colour and chefs figure out how many tiers to give their show-stopping cake. They look at the image that their mind is creating and then decide whether or not it 'looks' right.

Each time your child sits a spelling test, he's not simply remembering the correct way to spell each word from memory, he's also 'reading' the word from the image that his mind is giving him.

You can test this out. Next time you ask him to spell a word (even if it's a simple word such as his own name) also ask whether he's seeing the word in upper or lower case letters. Are the letters in colour or black and white? And can he spell it backwards?

You can track his eye movements as he's doing this and don't be surprised if uses his finger to actually point to what he's seeing.

To see this process in action more closely, watch the contestants' faces on a TV quiz show. As they're thinking of the correct answers, they'll be looking up. It could be to the left side or it could be to the right side depending on which part of the brain they're retrieving the information from. Some will look high up to the ceiling.

Perhaps you've noticed this in your own behaviour whenever someone puts you on the spot and asks you to give your children's dates of birth, your address or telephone number. We automatically look out ahead and maybe slightly up too. The information isn't 'out there', but it 'feels' as if it is.

Why is this important?

With a better understanding of how our minds work and how we use this clever retrieval system, you can check that the learning conditions at home are right for your child.

Does your child have a desk in his bedroom that faces a wall, for example? Some children need to 'see' a long way out in front of them in order to be able to see the answer clearly. Move the desk away from the wall and place it under a window instead. That way, your child will be able to look outside – as far as he needs to.

And the phrase *'Don't keep looking up at the ceiling – the answer's not up there!'* might sound familiar to you from your own childhood. It's common to hear teachers say this to their pupils and yet, they're wrong. The answer most probably, is up there. If your child is struggling to figure out a problem in their mind, encourage them to look up at the ceiling, to see if it would help. Looking down at a flat piece of paper doesn't encourage the creative juices to start flowing at all.

And if your child doesn't enjoy sitting at a desk, consider introducing a standing desk. These are much more suitable for restless children and a recent pilot study at a primary school in Bradford, led the teacher to believe that it improved concentration levels.

Exercise – The NLP Spelling Cure

Here's a very clever NLP technique that was developed by Robert Dilts. It will help your child with their tricky spellings:

1. Place the correct spelling of the word in front of you so you can see it easily.

2. Close your eyes and think of something that feels familiar and relaxing (a favourite teddy, vanilla ice-cream, the comfy beanbag in front of the TV). When the feeling is strong, open your eyes and look at the correct spelling for a few moments.

3. Next, move your eyes up and to the left (or to the right for left-handed students) and picture the correct spelling in your mind's eye.

4. Look up at your mental image and write down the letters you see. Check what you have written against the correct spelling. If incorrect go to step #1.

5. Look up at your mental image and spell the word backwards (write the letters down from right to left). Check the spelling. If incorrect, go to step #3

HELPFUL HINTS for using the 'Spelling Cure' include:

a. Picture the word in your favourite colour.

b. Make any unclear letters stand out by making them look different than the others in some way – e.g. bigger, brighter, closer, a different colour, etc.

c. Break the word into groups of three letters and build your picture, three letters at a time.

d. Put the letters on a familiar background. Picture something like a familiar object or movie scene then put the letters you want to remember on top of it.

e. If it is a long word, make the letters small enough so that you can see the whole word easily.

f. Trace the letters in the air with your finger and picture in your mind the letters you are writing. With long words, people often experience difficulty in being able to initially visualise the entire words easily (especially people new to the process of visualising). Most often what happens is that some letters are clear but the rest get out of focus or hazy. In such a situation one needs some operations to make the unclear letters stand out.

In this case there are two more sub-operations that may be used:

a) breaking the word down into groups of letters (typically groups of three)

b) changing some sub-modality quality of the letters that have been difficult to visualise in such a way that makes them stand out.

For instance the letters can be:

- made brighter
- put in one's favourite colour
- put on a familiar background
- made bigger, etc.

WORDS THAT WORK

Encourage your child and keep them calm by using phrases such as:

- *I can understand that you're feeling cross and annoyed about having to do this. Let's sit down together and figure out what needs to be done.*

- *Instead of just giving up when it started to get hard, you carried on and figured it out. That's great.*

- *I noticed that you went back and checked it over when you finished and spotted that mistake. That's progress. You can do it without needing me to remind you.*

- *Even though you were worried that you'd make a mistake, you took a sensible guess and it was right!*

- *You were able to sit really calmly today and it helped you to concentrate.*

Listen out for the type of vocabulary and language that your child is using in return. We already know that phrases such as: *I can't... I must ... I should...* suggest a problem. In particular, those types of phrases will be dampening your child's motivation and the whole task will feel a lot harder as a result.

Use gentle questioning to find out what changes could be made to make things easier. If a child says:

"I can't do my maths"

Rather than replying with:

"Stop moaning and get on with it"

Or

"When I was at school, I had my fair share of maths homework. I don't intend to do yours for you now"

Ask:

"What is it about this particular piece of homework that's stopping you? Last week's went really well, so there must be something in particular about today's that's a problem. Let's break it down into small steps and see what it could be."

EXAMS

Exams frighten almost everyone and today's students have to face more of them than any previous generation, so it's not surprising that stress and anxiety can begin to overwhelm even the most able.

Feelings of nervousness quickly lead to a lack of motivation to study and forgetfulness, followed by an inability to concentrate and think clearly. This leads to under performance and even failure, regardless of academic potential and ability.

According to the NSPCC there's been a 200% rise in requests for counselling as a result of exam stress with its ChildLine service receiving more than 34,000 approaches in 2013-14.

As parents we have an instinctive urge to keep our children safe and out of harm's way. Watching them struggle and cope with one of life's biggest challenges independently can be very frustrating. Some parents have overwhelming desires to 'do something' to help, but remember, a gentle prod can be helpful but a shove rarely is. It's time to play a more supportive role.

Of course, there's no substitute for real knowledge acquired throughout the academic year but when you reach the final hurdle, it's the little things that count; the difference that could make all the difference.

EXAM TAKING TIPS

Preparation is the key to success: Learning information and reproducing it accurately is, on the surface, what exams seem to be all about.

First of all, remember to keep your H. A. T. on. Or put more simply, if a child is *Hungry, Angry* or *Tired* revision will not go so well. Put these things right first and notice the difference it will make.

'**Junk food, junk mind'**: Children should be eating well at this time. If you want your mind and body to be working at its best, you need to think about the fuel that is being put into it. I remember receiving some exam advice from one of my children's schools and the advice was that children should eat what they like: if burgers and junk food are their favourite then there's nothing wrong with this throughout the exam period. I disagree completely with this. The exam period could last six weeks or more and eating nutritionally deficient foods for that length of time will not help them to pass. Remember, you're looking for ways to pick up extra marks here and there – the ones that your child usually misses out on. If your child's most difficult maths paper happens to be right at the end of the six week period, then having gorged on sugary snacks and sweets all that time is not going to help them to feel calm and concentrate easily. Read the diet tips in Chapter Four: Eliminating Fears and Anxiety, to get clued up.

Get moving: If your child shows clear signs of feeling grumpy or fed up with revision, encourage them to shake it out! Tell them to hop around on one leg and shake their hands in the air. Shuffling your circulation and energy flow around like this makes it harder for the body to hang onto negative feelings. Make sure they take regular exercise breaks from simple walks around the block to a couple of longer activities during the week. Studies show that children who do aerobic exercise such as cycling, swimming, playing football or running, achieve higher exam results.

Sleep: Ensure your child gets plenty of this and sticks to their usual waking and sleeping hours. Don't allow them to slip into holiday mode during study leave for it makes getting up for exam that much harder. This is especially important if they have an afternoon exam – they need to get up at their usual morning waking time in order to be in the best frame of mind.

Be aware of what works best: Everyone is different, so help your child figure out what does and does not work well for them. If they tell you they had a particularly good revision session, make a note of the details such as the time of day, the location, whether it was totally quiet or with background noise. Note whether they'd just eaten and notice the particular book or system that they were using. If it worked well on one occasion, the chances are it will work well again.

Work with your child to help them begin noticing how different revision styles suit different people. They may get on better:

- Recording their voice onto a tape recorder
- Using a whiteboard and coloured pens to group information
- Creating flash cards
- Using rhymes, mnemonics or mind maps
- Having someone to test them

Looking at two year's worth of Geography files can feel slightly daunting for anyone. Chunking it down into smaller sections and categories will make it easier to remember.

Choose revision surroundings carefully as the more these match the exam room environment, the better. Lying on a bed, or sitting in the garden under a tree may seem like a nice idea to make those hours of studying easier, but sitting at a table will help your child's body associate this position with their studies. Recalling the information in exam conditions will be a lot easier when they adopt a similar pose.

Tolerance levels for untidy bedrooms, loud music and grumpy moods need to be at their highest right now. Your priority is to keep everyone happy, so ease off and let things slip a little until the exam period is over.

Draw up a timetable of exams and study periods. Use a large piece of paper for this and remember to include the weekends and leisure activities too. It will feel less daunting to be able to see a few days of exams followed by a weekend, rather than a month's exams en masse. Stick it where your child will see it. They will be arriving and leaving school at random times now and it will be easy to get thrown by this.

Make time to sit and listen. As boring as it may be to listen to your child recite his French oral for the fifth time, grit your teeth and remind yourself it only happens once. Since you are taking an active involvement, it will be easier to encourage breaks from study with activities such as a meal out with the family. This will help break up the stress and relieve some pressure.

Keep your child happy and motivated – do everything in your power to keep things calm and positive – even if it means tolerating their choice of music playing at full blast in the car as you make your way to the exam! If they arrive in a happy motivated state this will serve them well.

Remember to use the 'Worry Box' technique in Chapter Four: Eliminating Fears and Anxiety if your child gets caught in a cycle of negative thoughts such as:

What if I fail? / I'm worried I might panic / I've forgotten everything.

To rid their mind of these thoughts, they should write them down on a piece of paper and then screw the paper up and place it in the Worry Box.

Encourage them to always say what they *do* want to have happen, rather than what they *don't*. For example;

- *I want to be calm and relaxed in the exam room.*
- *I want to pass my exams and go to University.*

Avoid rewards: Psychological studies have proven that offering rewards actually reduces the level of interest your child will have in their studies. They'll also send out the message that exams are negative experiences that need compensating for and you'll inadvertently exaggerate the unpleasantness of the whole situation. (You can read more about the negative effects of praise and rewards in Chapter 11).

The worst outcome would be that your child's attention and focus is taken off the task in hand and is placed onto the reward. In order to be successful, your child needs to have a clear picture of his goal and want it badly. Offering money in return for good results places your child's desire in the wrong place and make no mistake, your child will figure out how to obtain maximum reward for minimum effort.

SEEING IS BELIEVING

Remember, seeing is believing. If your child can create a very clear picture in their mind of what it is they want to achieve, that on its' own may well be enough to make the difference between success and failure. Remember, it's a technique that all top sportspeople use on a regular basis. Top footballers don't just *hope* they'll score goals – they have a very clear image of themselves scoring and this makes it that much easier for their bodies to produce the results.

The more powerful your child can make the images, the more motivated they'll find themselves each morning.

Exercise – Visualising Success

Read through this exercise with your child and then encourage them to practice this technique every day:

1. Close your eyes and allow yourself to imagine it is August. It's a hot, sunny day and you've arrived at school to collect your exam results. Are you alone in this image, or with someone else? Notice as many of the details as you can, even the clothes that you're wearing.

2. Become aware of any sounds in this image – it could be the sound of other people talking perhaps or music in the background.

3. Imagine you have a remote control in your hand and can make alterations to this picture: turn the colours up brighter, bolder, stronger and make the volume even louder.

4. You can even add your own soundtrack to this movie – your favourite tune.

5. Now, imagine you're walking into the school hall and are being handed a brown envelope. It is your exam results. Continue running the movie forward, feel yourself opening the envelope and reading the piece of paper within.

6. How would it feel if you could see exactly the results you'd been hoping for?

7. Read that piece of paper and see the grades you've wanted so very badly.

8. Really enjoy this image. Notice the expression on your face, the smile that tells you all is well. Make this picture a bit bigger and bring it even closer to you, turning up the volume and all the colours as you go. Enjoy it! This is your special moment and it can be yours.

Practise this each day and by the time your exams come round, you will have set your mind and body onto that path to success.

It's not uncommon today for some children to receive their results online – in which case, change all the details to suit. Encourage your child to see themselves waking up in the morning, walking over to the computer, logging-in and seeing just the results they had been wishing and hoping for.

DEALING WITH LAST MINUTE STRESS

At crucial moments, say in the last few hours before an exam, the stress may just get too much for your child. However, if you've worked your way through this book, practiced some techniques and planned ahead, you should be able to see them through the worst.

One of the most useful things to master is how to deal with any signs of a panic attack. It is well worth going back through Chapter Four to get some more tips on relaxation and in particular, revisit the breathing techniques. If your child feels panicky just as they're entering the exam room there's an easy solution. They should place their hands over their mouth and imagine they're blowing up a balloon, blowing out slowly for as long as they can.

This should be repeated three times. Explain to them that these panicky feelings are created by chemicals in our bodies and by doing this exercise they will have blown them right away.

To add to the calming effect they could repeat the following affirmation to themself:

"I'm starting to feel calm and relaxed, becoming more calm and relaxed with each moment…"

Their body will automatically follow the direction of their mind.

WORDS THAT WORK

- *It's not about being the best, it's about being better than you were yesterday.*
- *I'm not telling you it's going to be easy, I'm telling you it's going to be worth it.*
- *I can see that you put a lot of effort into that*
- *I know that you're doing your best*
- *Since last week, I've noticed a real improvement*
- *Look at the progress you've made, in spite of..*
- *You can start to feel proud of yourself..*
- *I can see that you're starting to feel more confident about…*
- *Each day you're becoming a little more…*
- *It's good that you're starting to realise…*
- *It's only natural that..*

WORDS THAT DON'T WORK

- *It's too late now*
- *Try your hardest*
- *So long as you try, that's all that matters*
- *I always hated Maths at school too*
- *I knew we should have got a tutor*
- *I told you to work harder*
- *How many times did I tell you to get on with your work*
- *You should have listened to your teachers*
- *Don't come crying to me now, it's too late*
- *If you pass your GCSEs we will take you to…*
- *Get five A* and we'll buy you…*
- *Don't worry*
- *There's no need to panic*
- *Grit your teeth and get on with it*
- *The teachers are all stupid*
- *Exams are a waste of time*
- *I've got enough on my plate without you adding to it*
- *See how many grey hairs you're giving me*
- *You'll regret not revising when you can't get a job*
- *Don't come crying to me when you're unemployed and miserable*

8

Fussy Eating and Mealtime Challenges

One of the most maddening aspects of modern life for countless parents is food fussiness. Millions of parents will recognize the feeling of despair when a lovingly cooked meal is met with tears and out and out refusal. As the inevitable, often near daily food fights end, the big question you'll have asked yourself over and over again is; what can you do?

As the mother of a child who was the fussiest eater on the planet (oh, you thought that child was yours?), I quickly learnt that there was little point pouring over one of the many recipe books on offer stuffed with healthy ideas to tempt kids to eat well. I pretty much knew I had as much chance of flying to the moon as getting my son to nibble on a cous cous and courgette bake, never mind eat anything other than fish fingers. Which he did pretty much every day for around ten years!

Children's fussiness is a very sensitive issue and as I realise now, the way to work through it is to break down the habits, behaviours and the anxiety that are associated with it. As well as thinking about what we put on our plates, we need to understand that when, how and why we eat, all have an impact on our children's view on food too.

Without perhaps realising it, we have more control over mealtimes than most of us think. In a sense, you're the director, conductor, or script-writer (however you like to picture it) of this particular scene and, as such, you can make a mealtime go any way you want. If you take control from the start, you won't be putting yourself into the position of becoming a fire-fighter later on, once it has all fallen apart in your absence.

Are you a good role model for your child? Are you constantly on a diet and worrying about your own food intake? Do you spend days on juice detoxes and saying out loud what you can and can't eat? Do you get transfixed upon which foods are good and which are bad? Even if your children are small, they will be listening and taking the information in. They will naturally follow your lead and will copy everything you do. And how consistent are you with table manners? If you lounge on the sofa with your feet up, licking the lid of a yoghurt pot, you can't expect your children to behave impeccably at the table.

Make mealtimes a family affair – It's not uncommon for busy parents to be tempted to sit their children down at the table, give them their food and then leave them to it. After all, the thinking goes, if they're competent enough with a knife and fork, this could free you up for a valuable half hour. It's very easy to slip off to wash up, empty the washing machine or make that urgent call once they're settled at the table. But is this rushing around setting the right example? If we do not value the dining experience, how we can expect our children to?

Create a calm, welcoming environment – Make use of relaxing background music, real tablecloths, napkins, flowers, jugs and placemats. Unless children are very young, I would avoid plastic. It simply encourages confusion between playtime and mealtime. Cups, plates and placemats made out of plastic festooned with cartoon characters, suggest to the child that mealtimes are just a game where 'mucking around' is acceptable. Instead introduce real china cups, glass jugs, proper stainless steel cutlery, china plates and so on as soon as possible. You'll find your children will behave better.

Laying the table can be turned into a learning experience for your child as the routine of folding napkins, pouring drinks from a small jug and laying cutlery develops their co-ordination, concentration and sense of order. It also means that your child's first encounter with the mealtime is not the moment at which they actually have to sit down and eat any food. They have time to become a 'participant' in the process beforehand.

Invite other guests on a regular basis and your child will come to see mealtimes as occasions for fun, rather than a battleground – and an opportunity to show off their table-setting and pouring skills.

Create a confident dialogue around food – Involve your child in every stage of the planning process around meals. Look at cookery books together, make shopping lists (encourage children to draw pictures on the shopping list), shop for food together and ask them to help prepare food and chop veg. While you do this, foster their sense of curiosity by exploring new foods as you look through books. Refer to these foods again as you go around the supermarket and let them pick up and touch them. Ask how they think they grow. Do they think it is a root vegetable, or do they grow on trees? If you don't know yourself, have a competition between you. Take a guess and then look it up online and see who was right.

Discuss your mealtimes in a Family Meeting – In Chapter 11, I discuss the concept of organizing a regular Family Meeting. This is the ideal place to discuss things such as menu plans and table manners, You can avoid correcting bad habits during mealtimes by addressing them in this meeting, creating a better atmosphere round the table as a result. Use this time to introduce new tasks such as pouring drinks, new items of cutlery, or demonstrating how to lay the table. You can allocate chores and duties during this time too.

Create a weekly menu plan with the family – Allow each child to choose their favourite meal and incorporate these into the timetable. Agreeing in advance what you'll be eating throughout the week will help you to stay calm, more organized and less likely to cave in to protests. Your child will learn that it's simply not possible to have their favourite dish every day, as you're accommodating everyone else's needs too. You'll be able to eliminate arguments by responding with:

"Yes, I know tonight's dinner is not your favourite but we all agreed we'd be eating this today at our Family Meeting – it's written down in our menu plan. Tomorrow, it's going to be your favourite dish, remember?"

Make a plan and stick to it.

Introduce themed dinners – Tasting new foods can be something that's enjoyed by all the family. The meal could be Chinese, Japanese, Mexican, French, or Italian. You can not only include unusual foods, but also play music and dress up accordingly whilst exploring the culture of that particular land. Invite friends and turn it into a party.

Create a starter – While you are busying yourself with the main event, place some ramekins in the centre of the table with a selection of chopped veg (such as carrots, mange tout, sliced avocado, cucumber, or beetroot) and dips. Each child could take a vegetable stick and get on with dipping whilst you're putting the finishing touches to the next course. You could even do this at breakfast time. This time the ramekin in the middle could hold pieces of fruit to be nibbled before their boiled egg and toast.

Create a tasting plate – offer pureed, tiny dollops of new foods going round the plate in a pretty pattern. Experiment with alternate colours and ensure there's one of each colour for each person at the table. Include adults in this game. Pass the plate around the table and each person uses their finger to scoop up the blob and eat it.

Present food on smaller plates – This will feel less overwhelming to your child plus, as soon as they start finishing everything on their plates, they'll come to see themselves as 'good eaters'. This would be progress indeed.

EXPLORING NEW FOODS

All too often we introduce a new food ready cooked, served up on the plate and then we stand over our children watching and waiting – will it be happily eaten or rejected outright? With this amount of pressure, it is little wonder children are unsure.

I feel it's best to explore new foods away from mealtimes and perhaps even the table – especially if sitting at the table is going to conjure up memories and feelings of arguments you've had over food before.

Be creative when it comes to exploring food away from the table – a picnic blanket in the garden or even on the sitting room floor is ideal. Follow these steps to help your child feel happier around food.

1.   **Show and tell.** Take turns to invite friends round and have exploration parties – ask them to bring really unusual foods. Talk about where in the world they come from and show pictures of the country of origin and the people. Fussy eaters get on better if sitting with their friends and will often try things they'd never countenance in the past.

2.   **Same but different.** Explore and discuss different varieties of the same product such as tomatoes. There are cherry ones, big red ones, yellow ones, green ones, plum shaped, big fat beef ones and those that are still 'on the vine' – and there are even some that have stripes like tigers! How are they the same and how are they different? Explore other foods that belong to the same group but are very different – eg: apples, berries, nuts, cheeses and breads. You can explore kiwi fruits by stroking and feeling their hairy skins brush against your child's cheek. Let them listen to what it sounds like when you rub the skin next to their ear. Cut one open widthways so they can see the seed formation and then cut another open lengthways so they notice how the seed formation looks different.

     Ask: *"What shapes and patterns can you see? How does it feel? Is it soft between the fingers?"*

And finally, very much finally:

"How does it taste? Some foods are soft and squidgy while some are hard and crunchy. Which is this one?"

Let them just explore and have fun.

3. **Guess the food.** Blindfold your child and ask them to explore foods on the touch and smell. What is the food? How do they know? If they don't like having a blindfold on, then use a small bag (drawstring washbags are good for this) to disguise the food and let them dip their hands into the bag and guess that way.

4. **Smelling jars.** Create a 'smelling game' by getting six identical containers or jars with lids that have small holes in the top – the ideal kind of thing would be ordinary salt and pepper shakers. Divide up your six containers to create three pairs. The idea of the game will be to smell each container in turn and find the other one that smells the same – creating a matching pair. Start by unscrewing the lid and inside each pair of containers place either a cotton wool ball soaked with something that's highly aromatic eg. coffee, peppermint oil, vanilla essence or use leaves from a scented herb eg. rosemary. Screw the lids back on and ensuring that your child can't see the contents of each container, shuffle them up on the table in front of you. Then invite your child to take a sniff of each container in turn through the holes in the top and find the one that smells the same. Once they've been sorted into pairs, you can remove the lids and look inside to see if they're correctly matched. This game will help those children who are very sensitive to smells and are put off foods by strong aromas – they'll become acclimatized to a variety of new smells.

5. **Get messy.** Some children don't like the feel and texture of slimy foods. For these children it is a great idea to involve them in messy activities elsewhere. Encourage them to try anything from playing with sand, finger painting or clay modelling.

6.   **Avoid silly games.** Don't encourage children to play silly games with food. Food is not a toy so should not be played around with as if it is a throwaway item. It's expensive and should be respected. Avoid doing things like making pictures by sticking pieces of fruit onto paper to make shapes and pictures of people or objects. Food is only there to get eaten.

GOOD NEWS ONLY

Have a house rule that only good news will get discussed at mealtimes – there'll be no moaning or whingeing. It's a habit that can be hard to get out of. We seem to naturally focus on the worst things that happened in the day.

- *The bus was late.*
- *I got a parking ticket today..*
- *I've got lots of work to do this evening..*
- *I had a horrible lunch at school.*
- *So-and-so pushed me over and I scuffed my arm.*
- *I came last in the swimming race.*

This type of conversation introduces an element of anxiety that will reduce your child's appetite and foster a sense of foreboding each time you all sit down together.

Aim to keep mealtimes positive, rather than laying the groundwork for them to become a complete battleground, for this sort of negativity instantly creates bad vibes around the table. Tension and stress reduces appetites and with a fussy eater in your midst that is the last thing you need.

Instead, encourage everyone to bring good news to the table, or to tell funny stories and jokes. Even if it means buying a joke book and each taking turns to read one out to the group. This way, only good feelings will be associated with the food that is being eaten.

Keep the language upbeat. Avoid using negative words and phrases such as *'no'* or *'don't do that'*. Instead say, *'let's do it this way'* or *'let's see if we can do this.'*

The most important attitude to take at mealtimes is for you, as a parent, to remain calm. Your child will not miraculously turn into the World's Best Eater over night and it is not fair to expect them to. By the same token though, stay positive and avoid falling into the trap of giving up too quickly – use your 21-Day Success Journal at the back of this book to help you stay on track and check out the relaxation tips I give in Chapter 12. Parents often withdraw food that has been offered and rejected and never cook it again. The train of thought is: if they don't like it now, they aren't going to like it next time. This simply isn't the case. Resolve to keep introducing rejected foods. If the child doesn't want to taste the food then encourage them to touch it, smell it, roll it between fingers and describe what they see. Again, it won't happen overnight, but you will see a change.

A FINAL NOTE

I mentioned at the beginning of this chapter that I was the mother of the fussiest eater on the planet – it's true. I understand how exhausting and frustrating this baffling and complicated problem is. George not only refused to eat a whole raft of foods but had such a sensitive sense of smell that he could be sick if he came anywhere near a pizza. It certainly made going to friends' birthday parties interesting. I remember one particularly embarrassing moment when we stayed in a hotel and the smell of fried breakfasts in the dining room proved too much for him. Cringe...

We consulted many 'experts' and were referred to psychologists at the local hospital – things really did get that bad. Did it make any difference? Not in the slightest.

By the time George was eight, I realised that things were never going to change, unless *I* changed. I decided to stop making it a problem, so that the problem would go away. And it did – things calmed down and got better.

I decided to respect his wishes and actually, respect him as another human being. After all, I didn't really know what was going on inside that head of his and perhaps, he did know what was best for him, after all. I made a promise to him that I would never make him eat anything he didn't want to – he had a fear of being 'tricked' or forced into eating something he didn't like. I would only serve him the foods he wanted to eat.

I guess I was lucky with the foods he would eat. He had hot chocolate made with fresh milk for breakfast and croissants, a bag of crisps and an apple for lunch – but only when he was at home. If he was at school he starved because they only offered cooked school dinners; packed lunches were not allowed. Then for his evening meal – well, it was fish fingers, peas and sweetcorn every day, including Christmas Day. For years and years and years. I felt I should have been on first name terms with Captain BirdsEye.

He loved eating oranges, lemons (including their skins) and apples but wouldn't go near a banana or nectarine. He wouldn't touch meat and particularly hated the sight of sausages, bacon and ham. He wouldn't eat eggs, cheese, butter or bear the smell of anything fried which would make him scream and hold his nose. This is with the exception of Pancake Day when, curiously, he managed to eat pancakes. Sooo annoying! He wouldn't eat bread, pasta, rice, salads, vegetables and pretty much everything else you'd find in a supermarket.

You had to admire his grit, his determination, the discipline and doggedness. He would not budge. I know he was hungry for much of his childhood, but he would not give in.

In return for my respecting his wishes, I asked that he respected mine. I didn't mind him eating fish fingers every day but I insisted they were eaten in a proper manner, at the table with a knife and fork and we invariably had Mozart playing in the background. I wanted him to sit at the table calmly without making a fuss or moaning – or worse, screaming and panicking if we were out eating at friends' or in a restaurant. Basically I wanted him to shut up. I'd had enough of it all. I didn't want to discuss it or talk about it any longer.

He agreed – we shook hands – the problem was gone.

All was quiet until he hit 13 years-old. He watched someone eating a steak and asked why I never gave him meat. I told him it was because he didn't like meat.

"But that's ridiculous," he said. "I've always liked meat."

What??? Being a Mummy is exhausting sometimes! And so the repertoire expanded to include steak and roast chicken. This kept him going until he left home.

Today, George is all grown-up. He's still a 'choosy' eater shall we say, shunning anything that's deemed unhealthy such as sausages, bacon, hams and dairy products. He adores eating salmon, sea bass, cous cous with roasted vegetables, steamed broccoli, avocados, falafels, nuts and seeds. He won't eat a sandwich but he'll have a hummus wrap. Basically, he's a bit of a health freak, passionate about keeping fit too. I envy the way he can be so disciplined and at the same time, find it irritating too.

Looking back on it, I think he knew what was right for him all along and we could have avoided those endless squabbles about food.

My advice to you now is this: focus on getting good habits and behaviours in place, for they are what will last a lifetime and become imprinted on the subconscious mind. You can change the menu later.

WORDS THAT WORK

- *As you become more and more relaxed about tasting new foods…*

- *I've noticed that as each day passes, you're becoming more and more interested in the different foods around us.*

- *I can see that you've been putting a lot of effort into laying the table nicely each evening with the napkins and cutlery lined up neatly. It looks good.*

- *And I have noticed how hard you've been working at carrying all the plates to the kitchen on the tray, after we've all finished eating. Thank you for that. You're getting stronger and carrying more and more each day.*

- *You're starting to enjoy tasting some of the new items on our menu plan. You certainly liked those sweet potatoes, didn't you? You've eaten them all up four times in a row now.*

- *It's good when you can behave politely and sit at the table till everyone has finished. I noticed you did this at Auntie Susie's and she was so pleased with you for doing that.*

- *I think you might be surprised to discover how quickly and easily you'll find yourself adapting to the new routine.*

- *That's great – you've already come up with three new ideas for the starters on our menu plan – I expect you can think of a few more too.*

- *Yes, I can understand that it can be a little tricky to begin with … And you'll soon get the hang of it.*

- *I already know that you're a really curious person who likes to try out new things – give examples: riding bikes; swimming; eating mushrooms…… so you'll probably be really curious about tonight's dinner…*

WORDS THAT DON'T WORK

- *You're such a good girl or boy.* This quickly becomes meaningless and will cease to have any impact on your child's behaviour.

- *Eat it all up.* This comes across as a command and will only create tension.

- *Just one spoonful.* Immediately suggests the food is not tasty.

- *Open your mouth: here comes the aeroplane / steam train / racing car.* No! Your child will grow up thinking you are stupid or at the very least, a liar.

- *Well done! Good boy!* Steer clear of overpraising a child simply for trying a new food. This sort of reaction immediately suggests it's a rare occurrence. You're trying to get to a situation where tasting new foods is a normal, everyday event.

- *Just try…* Never 'try' anything: see the Words that Work Chapter for more details about this.

- *Once you've tasted everything you can leave the table.* It's best to avoid bargaining and falling into the 'if you do this, then I'll let you do that' trap.

- *When you've finished up all your dinner you can have dessert.* What if your child is no longer hungry after eating dinner? It's so easy to overfeed our children nowadays, so be on your guard.

- *No dessert till you've eaten your dinner. Dinner first.* This is similar to above and immediately makes it sounds as if the dessert is the treat or reward for eating the dinner. Of course it will seem more desirable. Worse still, many parents will let their child leave the table to eat their dessert in more comfortable environment eg. on the sofa, in front of the TV. No wonder dessert tastes nicer!

- *You're not leaving the table till you've eaten everything up!* This phrase belongs to a time long gone – a time when food rationing was not uncommon. Nowadays we have problems with portion control with manufacturers and supermarkets encouraging us to serve larger and larger portions. Listen to your child and not the instructions on the side of the packet of food.

- *There are starving children in Africa.* This fact has no bearing on your child's appetite and will only make them think that you're not listening or respecting their needs. Don't be surprised if you're met with the response of: *Then send my plate of food to them – they need it more than me!* This, of course, gets you no closer to a resolution.

Other helpful resources – A Magic Day Out, Boost Your Confidence, Fussy Eating No More CD/MP3s available from www.success-4-kids.com

9

Junk Food Cravings and Weight Issues

Growing up in the 21st century with our excess of food – most of which is manufactured to look highly attractive but in reality is full of fattening, empty calories – is proving to be a complicated business for our children. The UK now has the highest rate of obesity in Europe with one in three children overweight or obese by Year 6 and, based on current trends, half of children will be obese or overweight by 2020[4].

Whilst some are growing up saddled with the health problems that come with being overweight, others are becoming addicted to their quick sugar fixes and learning that food is the quickest way to change unwanted feelings – be it anxiety caused by exams, boredom during long school holidays or tiredness caused by late night social media networking.

I can remember being asked by my 11 year-old daughter how old she would be when she had to start dieting – and this was before there was even a hint of excess flesh on her young body. The diet industry had done a brilliant job of brainwashing her into believing that our bodies grow into the wrong size and shape and that only by following the latest faddy diet will she begin to resemble 'normal'. She was astonished to discover that not everyone needs to go on a diet for as she pointed out, the shops are full of diet books and magazines – it's all anyone ever talks about.

---

[4]   Royal College of Pediatrics and Child Health statistics

I've long believed that this intense scrutiny of what we eat and endless diet talk means that rather than solving a problem, we're simply attracting more of it to ourselves. As I keep saying – 'what you see is what you get'. The more our minds are 'thinking fat', so it follows we become fat. If young children get the impression that dieting is inevitable, it's because they've learnt that growing fat is inevitable. The biggest danger facing today's children is perhaps not the fatty chips on their plates, but growing up in an environment that encourages them to believe that becoming overweight is a sad but inevitable fact of their lives.

Many parents feel, perhaps justifiably, that speaking to their children about weight is a bit of a minefield, even if they believe there may be a problem in this area. There are a lot of conflicting views in the media about food and diet so it can be hard to know what to think. The last thing any parent wants to do is to keep nagging their child about their food intake giving them a complex and adding to their problem.

The other side of this coin is the fact that young people today are very much aware of weight related issues. They can hardly fail to notice the media's obsession with thin (or over-weight) celebrities. Today, people are often celebrated more on how they look than on any other achievement.

We can none of us avoid the subject and hope it goes away. If your child has food issues, whether they are eating too much and are unhealthily overweight, or eating too little, it's good to talk. You may well dread the moment your offspring says 'am I too fat?' or 'does my bum look too big in this?', but it may well happen. You need to think carefully about how you would reply.

As parents it can be easy to think that saying nothing in particular, or sidestepping the questions will be better, as this will avoid hurting your child's feelings. But, if your child raises concerns about their weight, stop for a moment and ask yourself why they are thinking this.

Have they seen something on TV or read about it? Or has this come from teasing at school?

This is most certainly the time for a common-sense chat. Explain that a child's weight does naturally fluctuate. This is normal. They fill out and then shoot up, so reassure your child. It's quite usual for girls to compare themselves to others in the class. The most rapid change for a child's body is puberty and for a while there could be massive differences within a single class. Girls naturally double the amount of fat as they go through puberty while boys on the other hand put on more muscle. In a few years' time, these massive differences will have reduced and they'll look more similar to each other.

If your child has clear concerns, try to be honest and take an objective look at them. Have you had concerns about their weight gain? Don't stick your head in the sand thinking the problem might simply go away; 21st century living means we have far too much food in our society. If your child is overweight, it's the eating habits that you'll need to address and not the weight gain at this stage. Your conversation should focus on quantities, frequency and habits rather than weighing scales, podgy tummies and tight clothing. It doesn't need to get personal. Indeed, it shouldn't.

With younger children, you may wish to take a slightly different tactic. More children in the younger age groups (under 10s) are becoming conscious of their body image. It's another bit of childhood that's disappearing. If your young child brings it up, it's best to deflect it and give praise and encouragement in other areas. Focus on their strengths in sports, school work, hobbies and in generally being an all round nice, friendly, helpful person.

If you are truly worried about your child's weight, whatever their age, consult your GP or nurse for advice.

ARE YOU FEEDING YOUR CHILDREN TOO MUCH?

1. Scrutinise the size of the portion you're serving your child. If it is pretty similar to your own portion size, then it's definitely too much. Keep an eye on the size of plates you're serving meals on too, for these also are getting bigger.

2. Do you find yourself falling into the trap of making things 'equal' for your children in order to keep things 'fair'? I can remember a time when my children started to count the number of chips on their plates to check that they all had been treated equally. I hadn't given my 5 year-old daughter the same as her 10 year-old brother and had to explain that if I gave them all the same amount then it wouldn't be 'fair'. Being fair is giving each child what's just right for them. The story of Goldilocks and the Three Bears came in very handy here.

3. If your child doesn't seem very hungry for the next meal, it can be easy to think you have a picky eater on your hands, when in fact, your child might simply be getting too much food to eat. It's not unusual for children to be given snacks three times a day now when 40 years ago, it was just once.

4. If you insist your child cleans their plate and finishes everything that's on it you could be pressurizing them into eating food when they're no longer hungry. This is a bad habit to be teaching them and will probably stay with them for life.

5. Check if your child's clothes are getting tight in the chest, waist or around the bottom even though they haven't outgrown them height-wise. If weight is increasing while height is staying the same, it's an indication that your child could be eating too much. Keep an eye on this for a few weeks and see if it settles with a growth spurt.

WHEN IS A FOOD, NOT A FOOD?

The best way to give your child a head start on the road to healthy eating is to teach them to see food for what it really is – fuel and energy – nothing more and nothing less. Reality becomes distorted in a society in which food is too abundant. As the number of different uses and meanings that we attach to food increases, so does the quantity of calories. It's great to enjoy food and have fun, but beware of all the extra calories consumed if on too many occasions you use food inappropriately.

A food is *not* a food:

When it's a plaything or toy: The boundaries between food and toys are becoming increasingly blurred. Necklaces and bracelets of sugar sweets and toy-filled chocolate eggs not only take calories into the playground but make calorie consumption part of the game. Keep food and play separate. Avoiding the supermarket ham with smiley faces means your child is less likely to become confused about where eating ends and play begins.

When it's a gift: Boxes of chocolates, cakes and bottles of wine are an automatic choice of gift for most people. Over the years, as our wealth has increased, so too has our 'giving'. Where once receiving a box of chocolates might have been an annual birthday treat, the opportunities to give gifts just seem to keep on increasing. It's not uncommon now to see teachers receiving a mountain of sweets, cakes and chocolates as an end of term gift. A trip into your local greetings card shop will be a quick reminder of the number of anniversaries and festivals that we seem to like to celebrate. It's not useful for your child to grow up with the perception that marking each of these occasions requires a giving and consuming of additional calories. Now, more than ever we need to be thinking about alternatives such as: flowers, photographs, candles or nice things for the bath.

When it's a reward: A special treat should be just that; a 'treat'. Something that happens once in a special while. In fact, it's good to allow your child to have that special treat now and again, as it's at this moment that the subconscious mind can register that this is something that happens sometimes and NOT every day. Sugary sweets are increasingly becoming attached to effort or star charts as rewards. This actually isn't helpful, for many psychological studies have now proved that the best way to get your child motivated and achieving is to focus on the goal itself rather the 'prize' at the end of it.

When it's a commiseration: We all need cheering up from time to time, but preferably not with food. The parent who offers sweets to a child who's just grazed a knee may have found a quick and easy distraction, but the long-term effect will be to teach that a shot of sugar can fix feelings of pain and anxiety. When children grow up believing that it's possible to fix internal feelings with external means, they are facing problems in the future. Life does contain disappointments and children need to grow up seeing that chocolate cake is wonderful, but it won't fix that broken heart or get your job back. All it will do is add inches to your waistline.

Time to Celebrate! Think of a celebration and I'm sure you'll find yourself automatically thinking about food. Food has become an integral part of our most important occasions, be it parties, weddings, birthdays or the New Year. It's no surprise that eating certain foods can trigger off a set of good feelings that have nothing to do with exciting taste buds or filling stomachs.

Today's children are growing up in an environment where 'fun' is considered to be high on the priority list. And with that fun ... comes food. Think back to the number of birthday parties you attended in your own childhood and compare it to the number your child went to in just the last year or month even and you'll begin to get the picture.

We really have to change our way of thinking about how we create 'fun' for children if we are to avoid steering them toward the obesity trap. With parents working longer and longer hours the cash-rich, time-poor mums and dads of today naturally desire fun, happy times when they are with their children. Add in a few other ingredients that challenge families today more than ever, such as divorce and the breakdown of extended families and we begin to get a nice cocktail of guilt, tiredness, isolation: all of which can be instantly changed by FOOD.

During the first few years of life, before the age of 10, parents can teach their children good eating habits and influence their attitudes about exercise. Good teaching now will stay with them for the rest of their lives.

NON-DIETING WEIGHT LOSS TIPS

It's never going to be easy to take away your child's favourite snacks and desserts, nor swap their calorie laden pizzas and burgers for lighter options, so start with some non-dieting, weight loss changes first. Creating a more orderly, disciplined environment will put your whole family on the path to healthier eating and weight loss, before you even need to start thinking about making substantial dietary changes.

I have included some non-dieting weight loss tips to help you change your behaviour at home to modify the entire family's eating habits:

Clear your kitchen clutter: If work surfaces are cluttered up with the latest kitchen gadgets (especially those that rarely get used), as well as old newspapers, bills and piles of ironing, you will not feel inspired to cook healthy, balanced meals. Clear the decks completely and create a more calming environment for yourself.

Get organised: If you regularly come home from work to find dirty breakfast dishes, or even the previous evening's left-over dinner plates cluttering your work surface, this will not help you in the slightest. Kitchen cupboards and fridges that are full of half-eaten packets of out-of-date food will leave you feeling frustrated each time you search for ingredients. You'll quickly give up the idea of cooking healthy meals and reach for the takeaway menu or a microwave meal instead.

Pay attention! Children hear these words many times throughout their childhood. But teaching them to pay attention to the food they're eating is going to be one of the most valuable lessons in life and may even be life-saving. Life in the 21st Century makes it harder for our children to eat consciously. Everything happens that much faster, it's noisier and more stimulating. Living life 'on the run' means it's easy to eat wherever we happen to be at a certain time of day – in the car, on the bus. Rushing around means you can't properly pay attention to your body's signals when you're eating and that's why many of us gradually become one of those people who's never quite sure when they are hungry and when they are not. I say 'become' because children are born with a natural ability to recognise the signs of hunger and fullness. It's adults who go on to wreck this for children.

So what is conscious eating not?

- It's not in front of the TV.
- It's not standing up.
- It's not in the car, on the bus or walking down the street.

Conscious eating is not eating crisps straight out of the packet because as your hand disappears into the packet and then moves straight up to your mouth, you don't get a chance to see the food itself. And if you can't see it, as far as your brain is concerned, it just didn't happen.

Have you ever sat in the cinema with a bucket of popcorn on your lap and been surprised to find it's empty? Perhaps you even glared at your neighbour, feeling convinced that they'd sneakily had some, taking advantage of the dark. The fact is that when we're not consciously looking at our food, we do not feel as if we are eating it – it means we can accidentally wolf down mountains of food without realising it.

Variety is the Spice of Life: Shepherd's Pie on Wednesdays, sausages on Thursdays, fish on Fridays. Does this routine sound familiar to you? Without even realising, families who follow repetitive patterns of eating are also encouraging unconscious eating. Nobody questions, nobody asks. Without thinking about it, everyone eats the same thing each week. And if you get used to eating the same food, you very quickly get used to eating the same quantity regardless of whether you need it or not. Unconscious eating never leads to a feeling of fullness and satisfaction – only a desire for more food.

Make a Meal of a Meal: We know that 'hunger' can occur in the brain without a real sense of hunger in the stomach. It is sometimes talked about as an 'emotional hunger'. It is a hunger in the head rather than the stomach. It can feel like a powerful emotion. Our brains do the 'feeling' bit for our bodies. Thanks to advances in psychological knowledge, we now know, for example, that 'phantom limb pain' is something that is genuinely experienced by people who have lost a limb. It is strange to imagine – but it is possible to feel an itch on an arm or leg that's no longer there. It's our brain that does the 'feeling'.

In just the same way, it's not only our stomachs that experience a sense of fullness when we've been eating – but also our brains. This is why if you've been eating in front of the TV or in the car and on the run, your brain won't have registered it in quite the same way as if you had eaten consciously.

This also explains our increasing desire for spicier and stronger tasting foods – only a packet of monster pickled onion extra hot chilli spicy puffs is going to do the trick. The busyness in your mind prevents you from fully registering what's going into your mouth and if it hasn't registered in your mind, it won't be registering in your stomach.

So, it's important to "make a meal of a meal". Aim for an all round sensory hit – exciting each and every one of your senses. You need to see it, smell it, feel it and even hear it as well as taste it. This will make you feel more satisfied. Make the table as attractive as possible by using colourful napkins, attractive cutlery and crockery. How about some flowers on the table or maybe a candle? And what about the food – the colours, textures and aromas? Keep these interesting and exciting too.

If your child is playing Playstation, listening to his iPod, texting his friends at the same time as eating, I can guarantee that the food won't make the slightest impact.

Encouraging your child to eat consciously means creating a calm environment, so he can be fully aware of the food he is eating. It also means trusting your child's innate ability to decide for themselves when they are full and have had enough to eat.

Limit TV viewing: We're familiar with the advice that eating in front of the TV is a complete no-no, but research shows reducing the number of hours a child is allowed to watch TV or play computer games in general, does in fact aid weight loss. Keep this activity to a maximum of two hours per day but preferably less.

Regular and adequate sleep: Many studies now show that sleep-deprived kids are susceptible to putting on weight. Bedtime is bedtime. Accept no nonsense. Many parents tell me they struggle to get their kids into bed, but the more confident you can be about the rules you're laying down, the more likely your children are to do as they're told. Being 'firm' doesn't have to be 'mean'. You can still be the sweetest, loveliest, cuddliest parent in the world: it's just rules are rules.

Remove TVs and electronic gadgets from the bedroom: I am not a great fan of TVs and computers in children's bedrooms. Nowadays it's easy to become overloaded with electrical gadgets if we include clock radios, mobile phones, TVs, Playstations, computers and tablet devices.

Scientific experts are beginning to agree that sleeping in an electromagnetic field does not aid restful sleep. I would recommend clearing the 'energy space' in your child's bedroom as much as possible by removing as many electrical items as you can. Read more about managing Screen Time arguments in Chapter 3.

Get organized with shopping: Plan your menus for the week ahead, make a detailed shopping list and avoid shopping when you're feeling hungry or tired. You'll find it easier to avoid buying too many of those high-calorie snacks that have a habit of creeping into the shopping trolley. And if they're not in the house, your children won't be able to consume them.

Engage in activities, sports and healthy exercise: Doing things together will show your child that you actually enjoy their company and want to spend time with them too– this will boost their self-esteem and help them to feel that making lifestyle changes are a joint venture.

BREAK TIME – THE MONTESSORI WAY

As Principal of my own Montessori school I know one of the most surprising features for prospective parents when they came to visit, was our Break system. Traditional nursery schools would have a fixed time for Break – usually around 10.30am. But following the Montessori programme meant our children had the freedom to make their own choices about when and how much to eat.

A selection of chopped fruit and milk was available throughout the morning. Each child had the freedom to choose when to take their break and sit at the little break table, which could seat just three at a time. I was aware that some children were up very early in the morning, perhaps eating breakfast at 6.30am whilst others could be spotted quickly finishing off their breakfast in the car as they pulled into the car park, around 9.15am.

Imposing a rigorous timetable on such young children, would mean some going hungry, whilst others would be eating when they were not. I wonder how many nursery school age children are eating food because they are being told to? Children are born with an in-built mechanism for detecting hunger and it's up to us adults to recognise this and trust their judgements a little more.

What also surprised and occasionally concerned parents was that we allowed the children to serve themselves – they could decide whether to have large or small portions. Because this was part of our normal routine, there was no novelty attached to the system. All the children were therefore able to behave responsibly, make good decisions and listen to their own hunger signals.

WHO'S WATCHING THE KIDS?

Of course, it's a lot easier to provide the right sort of environment to ensure your children eat slowly and consciously if you are around to keep an eye on them. But as more and more families have working parents, it's not uncommon to have children, especially teenagers, arriving home from school before Mum or Dad.

It's during this 'after school / before evening meal' period that boundaries can begin to slip away. Left to their own devices, teenagers can quite easily munch their way through a week's supply of snacks and drinks whilst happily lying on the sofa in front of the TV.

It's not easy to get your kids to behave the way you'd like them to, from a distance. Or is it?

If you've repeatedly made it clear what the boundaries are with regards to after-school snacks to no avail, my advice to you is "save your breath". Far more persuasive than your words will ever be is, actually, a mirror.

It's been proven that people behave in more socially desirable ways when they can see their own reflection in a mirror. Arthur Beaman, an American Social Scientist, together with his colleagues, carried out a Halloween experiment monitoring 'trick or treaters' visiting 18 different houses.

As a group of children visited each house in turn, they were told they could help themselves to sweets from a large bowl that was positioned in the hallway. The adult would then make some excuse and leave the hall reminding the children that they could have only 'ONE' each. And then the children were spied upon through a peephole. Of course, because they thought that no-one was looking, the children took more than one each and in some cases, big handfuls.

Then in the second part of the experiment, a big mirror was placed next to the bowl of sweets. As before the children were left alone in the hallway of each house and told they could help themselves to 'one' sweet only. This time, as they were spied upon, it was clear that because they could see their own reflections in the mirror, they behaved really well and in fact, did only help themselves to one sweet each.

This same experiment was repeated in many different situations. For example, with a group of adults leaving coins in a container as payment for cups of coffee. The researchers got the same results. When people saw their own reflections in a mirror they behaved more honestly, in a way that was more socially desirable. They were less likely to do wrong.

You can try this experiment for yourselves at home. Position mirrors or mirrored tiles in the locations most likely to present challenges for your children, for example, inside the cupboard where the biscuits are kept or in the fridge – notice how their behaviour changes over time. In fact, try it on yourself!

If mirrors aren't available, further research showed that this works equally well with large pictures of eyes – perhaps you seen these cleverly positioned in underground car parks and subways?

Ordinarily, we use mirrors to see what we look like on the outside, but this study also proves that when we see our reflections, we are also looking at what we look like on the 'inside'. And if our perception of our inside self is of someone who behaves well or someone who desires to behave well, then watching our reflection will encourage us to behave in a way that will match.

WORDS THAT WORK

- *At the moment, it's possible that you've put on some extra weight, but pretty soon you'll discover that your height will catch up.*

- *I think you'll be surprised at how easy it can be to make changes and swap the fizzy drinks for water. I think you might surprise yourself the most of all, don't you think?*

- *Listen, you may not know exactly what to do right now, but not having the solution can make you feel more determined.*

- *Feeling frustrated and upset is quite natural and usually it encourages you to think up of ways you can do something about it.*

- *As you're coming to the dinner table, turn off the TV please,* is more likely to be met with compliance rather than a straight *Turn off the TV.*

- *So, you've been feeling worried about your weight – to make yourself aware that you need to do something about all the fizzy drinks you're having.*

- *I get it – you've decided that you don't like any of the vegetables that we eat at home – in order to start experimenting and tasting some new ones.*

- *I, like you, completely get how nice it is to eat sweet, sugary snacks… and that's why we can bake a cake on Sunday.* (rather than eat one right now).

- *So, it's possible that you could start making the changes we've talked about; which will you probably do first, do you think?*

WORDS THAT DON'T WORK

- *You always stuff your face with biscuits when you come home from school*
- *You never eat healthy foods like vegetables*
- *Keep eating pizza and you'll end up looking like a pizza*
- *It's not your fault – you're just the chubby one in the family*
- *You've got big bones*
- *How much more food are you going to eat?*
- *Don't you think you've had enough?*
- *Don't come crying to me when you can't find a dress to fit you for the School Prom*
- *Oh, don't worry – you'll be fine*

Sleep and Bedtime Problems

Of all the daily arguments in the home, bedtime flare-ups are one of the most common. Young children, in particular, are prone to meltdowns at this time. Late in the evening both parents and children are running low on patience, or the capacity to cope. You're more likely to snap and give vent to your frustrations and you'll be convinced your kids are doing their best to wind you up. From their point of view, they are not being 'difficult', they simply don't feel the need to go to bed.

The stage is set for an epic battle of wills and the knowledge that you are going to have to go through the whole sorry experience the next night, makes it even harder to bear.

Most people understand that children need a good night's sleep to have a happy and healthy life. Poor sleeping patterns in children can lead to poorer achievements at school, behavioural problems and obesity for they'll start craving sugary, starchy foods, as well as sleep deprivation for the whole family.

If you are not sure on how much sleep constitutes a 'good night's sleep', the following table shows how many hours they should be getting according to their age.

Sleep duration[5]:

Age (years)	Recommended quantity of sleep
1	Day: 2hr 30 mins Night: 11 hrs
2	Day: 1hr 30 mins Night: 11hrs 30 mins
3	Day: 0 to 45 mins Night: 11 hrs 30 mins / 12 hrs
4	11hrs 30 mins
5	11hrs
6	10hrs 45 mins
7	10hrs 30 mins
8	10hrs 15 mins
9	10 hrs
10	9hrs 45 mins
11	9hrs 30 mins
12	9hrs 15 mins
13	9hrs 15 mins
14	9hrs
15	9hrs
16	9hrs

---

[5]   Source: www.nhs.uk

Establish a proper bedtime routine: If you're struggling to do this, it will help to write out a timetable showing the exact time for tidying up, going upstairs, laying out school things, bathing, teeth brushing and reading a story, right up until 'lights out'. Write the schedule on a large piece of paper and put it somewhere your child can see it. If everyone knows what they're supposed to be doing, they'll be fewer arguments. If your child is unhappy with some element of the routine then you can agree to discuss it at the next Family Meeting (Chapter 11), but in the meantime the schedule needs to be followed. Stick to the rules: you need to create good habits in your child's mind and remember, habits stick! Be consistent and do the same thing each night for at least a week and you'll see things starting to change.

If, after a week, you find you are still struggling to get your kids up to bed, start the routine earlier.

It can be tempting to allow a child who's nervous about going to sleep, (maybe because they're afraid of the dark, or regularly suffer from nightmares or night terrors) to have a staggered bedtime routine with some time spent unwinding and snoozing on the downstairs sofa once they're ready for bed, but this could be making your child's problem worse. They'll find it increasingly difficult to get into the habit of falling asleep independently and you'll be forever stuck with them on the sofa. They need to learn how to lie in bed and fall asleep naturally. (Check out the 'Magic TV Control' technique in Chapter 4 if your child has fears at night-time.)

We've all fallen asleep in front of the TV before, only to wake up feeling disorientated and then we struggle to get to sleep when we do actually go to bed. It disrupts the pattern of our sleep cycle and if this regularly happens to your child it only adds to your bedtime troubles.

Keep the bedroom tidy: It's not relaxing for a child to sleep in a room that has dirty clothes, toys, books and shoes strewn all over the floor. We all feel calmer in an uncluttered environment and the tidying up process can become an automatic part of the bedtime routine. It will signal the 'end of the day'.

Is the room is too light? It's better to sleep in a dark environment because light and hormones dictate our sleep patterns. When light dims in the evening, we produce a chemical called melatonin, which gives the body clock its cue telling us it's time to sleep. The sooner you can train your child to sleep in a dark room so much the better. There's a trend to have night-lights on in bedrooms to help children fall asleep. I say 'trend' because these haven't always been available and I do wonder if the manufacturers are taking advantage of selling us yet another gadget. Wean your child off these as soon as you can by taking small steps to making the room darker each night until you remove the light completely. And do make use of blackout blinds in those light summer evenings.

Avoid electronic gadgets: Having items like mobile phones, laptops and iPods recharging near the bed is not a good idea, for the electro-magnetic field created by these stimulates the mind and will keep your child awake. And, if they're awake in the small hours of the morning, the temptation to go on to social media and chat to friends will be too great if the phone is under the pillow. Likewise, it's better not to have TVs and DVD players in the room; bedrooms are for sleeping and relaxing in. This may be tough for your child but it's important for good health.

Create a 'Worry Box': Too often the first opportunity to think about worries is at the end of the day, when our minds are starting to slow down. Don't be surprised if your child starts blurting out their problems at bath time. This can leave some children 'wound up' just when you want them to be winding down. Work with them to write each worry down on a piece of paper and put into a Worry Box. (See Chapter 4 for full details) Psychological studies show that this works by tricking your mind into thinking that the worry has been dealt with. Let your child open their box once a week and look back to see how many of those 'worries' actually went away naturally or even needed to be have been worried about in the first place.

DEALING WITH A CHILD WHO WON'T SLEEP ALONE

You'll find there's often conflicting advice offered to parents for dealing with children's sleep problems. This is because there's no 'one size fits all' answer – a two year-old crying in a cot because he hasn't yet learnt how to fall asleep alone, is very different to an eight year-old say, who is afraid of the dark and having nightmares.

I hear many stories of parents spending a whole evening sitting in a child's room just waiting, praying for them to fall asleep. And rather ironically, the longer we sit, the longer it takes.

Rather than inducing feelings of security, this actually does the reverse. It encourages your child to feel more anxious, thereby staying awake for longer. The child can never quite be sure when, or if, you're going to leave, because most parents promise dearly that they'll stay. Of course, eventually they will leave so naturally, children start wondering if they can trust their mother or father again. So they test it out again the following night and the night after that.

Breaking bad habits may take as long as a month, but do resolve to do it. It will be kinder and better for your child who will get a better night's sleep, feel more connected and happier – and so will you. Keep a diary to track your progress. It's not uncommon for parents to give in after a week or so, convinced that they've made no progress whatsoever when in fact, they have. Use the 21-Day Success Journal at the back of this book to help you.

GRADUAL WITHDRAWAL
(More suitable for slightly older children)

Begin by talking to your child about the problem and reassure them that you do understand how they feel and you'd like to help them feel more comfortable at night time. Introduce a story of another little child you knew that also had this problem or you can invent (if needs be) a story from your own childhood of how your sister/brother/friend fixed this particular problem and how much happier they felt when they finally did – for life became so much better afterwards.

Introduce the idea that certain things are appropriate at certain ages. For example:

"Once upon a time you couldn't walk and you couldn't talk and now you can do those things easily."

Highlight things that they'd yet to learn in the past:

"When you were five years old (adjust the age to suit) you couldn't read a book or write your name, but now you can do those things so well. It just took a little bit of time to learn how to do them. And learning how to stay in bed alone, falling asleep comfortably is just one more of those things that you can easily do. And we can start practising right now..."

Reinforce your statements by discussing the 'benefits' of this new pattern of behaviour. *"Once you've learnt how to stay in bed and fall asleep easily all by yourself, you'll be able to invite a friend over for a sleepover. I wonder which one you will choose to invite first."*

If your child is anxious about going to bed alone, commit now to never lying down on the bed with your child again if this is what you've been doing. For a start, it's too easy to fall asleep yourself and it's time to be taking steps away from snuggling up with your child. I can appreciate this might be tough for many working parents in particular, who perhaps haven't seen much of their children throughout the day and this time spent together is precious. However, remind yourself of the longer term benefits. Once you've cracked the problem, you'll be able to lie back down with them once more.

For now though, to begin to break the habit, substitute lying next to your child with kneeling alongside the bed. At this stage you can have your arms around them in a cuddle too. Once your child has got used to you being off the bed rather than on, begin to reduce the cuddling to simply touching. Keep this up for a few days.

The next step is to take yourself further away from the bed perhaps by placing a small chair nearby and sitting in it. Now you can be close enough for your child to touch you and you can stop touching them. Gradually move your chair further and further away till you are sitting by the door and then eventually sitting outside the bedroom in the hallway (you can keep yourself busy by reading a book or catching up with emails on your laptop). Keeping the steps that you take really small, will mean that your child will notice the separation less. If they begin to cry you can reassure them with your words, but don't be tempted to slip backwards nearer the bed, but take this as an indication that you may have moved too quickly. You could also distract your child by occupying yourself with tidying the room and folding clothes. Now and again say something like:

"I must just go and bring the clean laundry upstairs."

Then gradually create longer separations.

As I said, this whole process could take a month to complete and it may well feel like it's the longest month of your life, but keep reminding yourself of the alternative. This clingy bedtime behaviour could easily go on for many more years if left unchecked. Just think how many evenings you'll need to give up for that. Use the Success Journal at the end of this book to keep yourself on track.

IMMEDIATE WITHDRAWAL
(More suitable for toddlers and younger children)

And what if the above method really doesn't work for your child – perhaps you've already tried the 'slow withdrawal' approach to no avail. Then, of course, there is the 'other' way – the one that many of us don't like to talk about. That is to get firm, lay down the law, shut the bedroom door firmly and ignore all your child's cries, screams and protestations. Most of us hate this method for it seems so cruel and you certainly need nerves of steel to listen to all that crying without caving in and going in to give a cuddle. But for some children, being cruel to be kind might be the only way. And many parents report having good results with this method, in just a couple of days.

However, this method can sometimes fail because parents give in after a few days, adding to the child's feelings of anxiety and confusion. One day, Mum or Dad is a cuddly parent on the bed and the next, they're marching out of the room, dishing out orders and refusing to engage with the child. Then a few days' later, they sheepishly come back and apologise for having done that.

But, if you do feel that the 'grit your teeth and leave your child to cry' method might be your only hope, then my advice is to be prepared - start planting the idea that you will be leaving your child to sleep alone, well in advance and before you actually start to leave.

Children will often ask the question *"You won't leave me, will you?"* and most of us will answer *"No, of course I won't – don't worry, I'm here"*. It's never going to be easy to leave after that. It's best to answer that question more honestly with *"I will one day... because all children sleep happily in their beds with just their teddies for company. And I know that one day, when you're ready... and not before... you'll be happy to sleep with just your teddies too. In fact, I've a feeling you'll be getting pretty fed up of me being here before long because you'll be busy talking to and cuddling them instead."*

You can continue to plant more ideas with presuppositions such as *"When you... "* or *"Once you..."* (sleep by yourself / want me to go...) and as before, follow up with those subtle reminders that 'things change all the time': *"Once upon a time you couldn't walk / hold a spoon / drink from a cup / go to the toilet alone – but now you can do that so very easily. You see, your body is changing and growing all the time and pretty soon, you'll find sleeping without me alongside you, so very much easier to do."*

You can spend a couple of weeks on this stage and gather proof and evidence that children all over the world sleep very happily by themselves using a friend as an example. Next time you're in the company of friends, ask their children if they sleep happily by themselves. Of course, you will only do this if you know for certain that they do! And when they answer that they do, you can find out what makes them feel happy to sleep alone – ie. their little bedtime rituals. Your child will be listening to this and those seeds will continue to be planted in their mind. Perhaps they'll want to adopt the same rituals – after all, the proof and evidence that they work is plain to see.

You could go as far as setting a time scale – eg. *"I can see that each day you're getting closer and closer to being ready to tuck down into bed by yourself... you won't be needing me soon"*. And then... *"in fact, I think you'll be ready for this next week – don't you think? It could be Tuesday ... or it could be Wednesday... but yes, I can see each day we're getting closer"*.

As I said at the start, every child is different so listen carefully to your child's response – your comments are designed to induce feelings of security, not anxiety.

And then for the final stage of leaving your child (and letting them cry if they have to) it often helps to invite a 'supporter or buddy' along for yourself. Think about whether you or your partner would benefit from having a friend or grandparent to sit with you and keep you company through the difficult part of ignoring those cries. Once you've made up your mind that leaving your child is the way forward, then consistency is going to be the key to success. Changing your mind and giving in after a couple of days can be harder for your child to deal with and won't get you any closer to your goal.

OLDER CHILDREN AND TEENAGERS

This next exercise is an ideal technique for kids who can't get to sleep because their minds are racing too much from a busy day, doing their homework, playing computer games, or chatting on social media. Read this exercise through carefully before you guide your child through it.

Exercise – Now I Can See

Ask your child to **close their eyes** and describe whatever comes into their mind, starting each sentence with *'now I can see'*. For example:

- Now I can see a big bowl of my favourite ice-cream.

- Now I can see my classroom at school and the maths lesson I had today.

- Now I can see the dog running around the garden – and I can hear his barking…

- Now I can see the pizza we had for dinner this evening.

- Now I can see the beach where we went on holiday last year.

It doesn't matter how ridiculous the things that he's "seeing" and describing are. Just encourage him to continue describing them in a continuous stream with a monotone voice. There is no rush to do this – slowly and steadily is the way.

Once your child has got the hang of doing this, ask him to do this silently – so he's describing what he sees to himself only. Ask him to slow his internal voice right the way down, so it's becoming a relaxing monotone just droning on, taking a deep breath and pause between each new thought. The tone of our internal dialogue has a powerful effect upon our feelings and the more it slows down, the more your child's thought processes will begin to slow down too. Pretty soon, as the mind begins to simply drift, rather than think, nodding off to sleep will be inevitable.

Encourage your child to continue doing this over and over, making the voice as boring and monotonous as possible until he or she falls asleep.

TEENAGE SLEEP ISSUES

I wanted to end this bedtime piece with a short section on teenage sleep problems. It's a myth that teenagers are lazy and sleeping for far too long. In fact, today's teenagers get far less sleep than previous generations. Not only does this leave them feeling tired but also leads to weight gain and impacts academic studies.

If you have a teenager who's struggling to sleep at night, don't be tempted to allow them to download a Sleep Measurement App on their phone. These work by placing a mobile phone under the pillow at night, so that it can record how often you toss and turn in your sleep and deduce from that your sleep cycle. It's interesting to know this, but counter-productive in the long run. Not only is it not a good idea to have an electronic gadget under your pillow emitting signals near your brain at night, but it can also act as proof and evidence that there's a sleep problem. Your child will come to you in the morning saying *"see, see, I told you it's impossible for me to sleep at night"*. They'll slowly brainwash themselves into believing they're a poor sleeper and it will become harder to reverse the problem.

The solution to help teenagers adjust their sleep patterns is to avoid long lie-ins at the weekends and spend more time outdoors. Exercising in the fresh air is good for encouraging deep, restful sleep. If your child is reluctant to go to bed at night, or struggles to fall asleep, do consider introducing more time outdoors.

Be aware of the arousing effects of fizzy energy drinks, caffeine (even in coffee-flavoured desserts and ice-creams), sweets, chocolate, sugary snacks, red meat and cheese. If your teenager is struggling to sleep at night, consider reducing these foods and drinks and add alternatives that contain the amino acid tryptophan which aids sleep. This would include turkey, milk, yoghurt, fish, poultry, eggs, bananas and mangoes. Eating more fresh foods and fewer processed ones will help too.

Encourage your child not to spend too much time 'awake' in or on their bed. If they often sit on the bed to play games, read books, study or listen to music, an association between bed and being awake is being made. This isn't a problem for those children who fall asleep easily but if your child struggles, then consider breaking this habit. If the bedroom really is the only place they can do all these activities then consider getting a comfy chair in the corner, or a beanbag on the floor. Beds are for sleeping in.

WORDS THAT WORK

- *I really enjoyed our special bedtime stories*
- *I can see that you're starting to feel sleepy… very sleepy in fact*
- *You're so special to me*
- *I really love you*
- *Do you want to pick up the toys off the bedroom floor **before or after** you've had your bath?*
- *I know that sometimes going to sleep alone can be a struggle for you, and that's ok because we don't have to be perfect all the time. But as each day passes, you'll be able to start noticing how much easier this is becoming for you*

WORDS THAT DON'T WORK

- *If you'd started your homework earlier we wouldn't be in this rush right now* – Bedtime should be a special one-to-one time; it will give your child something to look forward to. This is not a time to remind your child of all the things they should have done – do that another time.

- *I want you to tidy up this mess when you get home from school tomorrow* – Best to leave those thoughts for tomorrow.

- *If you stay in bed and go to sleep by yourself, you'll get sweets in the morning* –Rewards are not appropriate for dealing with this problem. Your child is not being naughty, he might just be feeling anxious. The promise of treats and goodies several hours hence will not allay his fears.

- *You're giving me a headache* or *I've had a hard day at work and I just want to go downstairs and sit down* – Making children feel guilty rarely works, it just upsets them more.

Other helpful resources – Sleep Soundly and The Sleepyhead Garden CD/MP3s available from www.success-4-kids.com

SECTION THREE

PUTTING IT INTO PRACTICE

11

Your Parenting Toolkit

We're now getting close to the time when we can begin to tackle the specific problems that you've been struggling with. You've now got some extra knowledge about words and phrases that work (and a few that definitely don't) and how to apply them to specific problems.

Before we dive in and start tackling some of these problems, I'd like to arm you with a few additional tools and techniques to see you through the transition to a more harmonious, happy family life.

As with many of the techniques outlined in this book, you may not need them all, or you may need one at a particular moment and then never again, but it is useful to have them at hand, should you need a little help, or feel your motivation to change things beginning to flag.

1) WHAT EXACTLY IS YOUR PROBLEM?

First things first – where are you going to start? You may perhaps be fully aware that things aren't running as smoothly as they could be, but often it's a little harder to get clear on exactly what changes are needed and when and how to begin. The following exercises are designed to help you get clear on these issues.

PART ONE – THE PARENTING WHEEL

In this section, you'll find a wheel that's been divided into segments and each segment represents a topic or group of topics – the kind of thing that you may be finding a challenge with your children.

I've chosen these areas because they're the ones that I'm most often asked for help with by my clients. You'll have also seen that these topics feature in separate chapters earlier on in the book where I give tips and advice for each problem, before demonstrating how best to put your 'magic words' into action.

Of course, these headings are just my suggestions and you may find it appropriate to change them – for example, if you're a teacher, then you can change the topics and apply the wheel to your class rather than your family. Likewise, it's possible to change all the headings and use the Wheel to look at just one child in particular, rather than the overall picture – each segment can represent an area of skills and personal development.

a) Tantrums, Rows and Flare-ups
These can be tantrums in the supermarket, arguments over screen time, sibling rivalry or any other kind of general arguments that crop up over being tidy and organised.

b) Fears and Anxiety
Does your child have a fear of the dark, or a phobia of dogs, spiders and things that go bump in the night? If these were dealt with, would life become easier for you all?

c) Confidence
Could your child do with an extra dose of confidence? Does shyness and embarrassment hold them back from displaying their talents on stage, in the classroom or on the sports field?

d) Habits and Behaviours
Does your child's thumb-sucking, nail-biting, hair-pulling or

bedwetting drive you mad? Have you noticed that the more you tell them to stop, the more they seem to do it?

e) School, Homework and Exam Stress
This segment could include getting ready for school and organizational skills as well as homework routines, study and exam stress.

f) Mealtime Challenges and Eating Issues
Is your child a fussy-eater or perhaps addicted to chocolate and sweets? Are you worried that they're eating too much, or perhaps too little? Is it simply a struggle to get them to sit at the table and behave well?

g) Sleep and Bedtime Problems
Under this section you can include general bathing routines, ease of getting children up to bed, tidy (or untidy) bedrooms, ability to stay in bed alone, quantity of sleep, getting up in the morning.

h) Self-care and Personal Development
This area is all about YOU – for happy parents and teachers produce happy, productive, successful children. Are you happy with the amount of looking after yourself that you're able to do? Do you have enough time to fit it all in? And what about skills and knowledge? Do you feel you would benefit from learning new things? Should you consult an expert.

Step 1: Start shading in each segment, from the middle of the wheel at zero and working your way out towards the number ten, which you'll find on the outer edge. How satisfied overall are you with this area? This first activity is all about getting a flavour or a feel for how things are in your life right now.

Step 2: When you have given each segment a score, think about each of the categories, one at a time and ask yourself this – if everything in this area was simply brilliant and deserved a score of ten, how many other categories would benefit as a result? Give each category a second score in this way.

YOUR PARENTING WHEEL

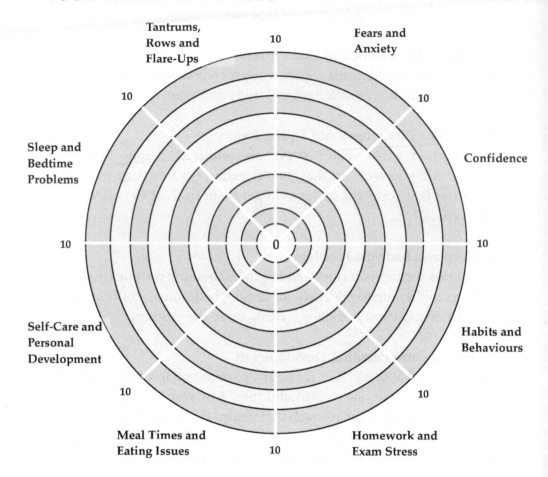

So, for example, if one child is reluctant to fall asleep independently each evening and you have to sit with them, then solving this one problem could mean that there would be many other benefits too. Perhaps you'd be able to supervise older children's homework; cook a healthy evening supper for yourself and your partner; go to a Yoga class for yourself.

Likewise, sorting out one child's fussy eating might mean an overall improvement in their relationship with siblings; supermarket shopping would be easier as would cooking meals, plus you'd be able to eat out more often in restaurants or visit friends for dinner.

So just one small change might have a beneficial knock-on effect on other areas.

To help you further with this analysis, take a step back from your wheel and notice how even or uneven the shaded areas make your 'wheel' look. If this were a real wheel, how easily would it turn? Would a gap in one part of it make it wonky and uneven? This is a clue to where you need to do the most work.

PART TWO – YOUR WISH LIST

Now that you've had a moment to reflect on the general feel of things, it's time to get more personal and more specific.

You know which areas 'generally' could do with a little attention, but what specifically and how specifically would you change things to make life better for you all? Take a few moments to think about what would need to happen to push the scores on the segments in your Wheel, up to the number ten.

I've created this Wish List with 25 spaces, but that does not mean you need to stop there – continue to make it as long as you feel is necessary. If you have a large family, it's possible your list will be twice as long.

For example, if your problem area is 'bedtimes', think about the details – what specifically needs to change? Is it the bedtime routine? Does one child need to go to sleep earlier – or perhaps for longer? Break each problem down into the individual bits that will need changing.

WISH LIST

1.	
2.	
3.	
4.	
5.	
6.	
7.	
8.	
9.	
10.	
11.	
12.	
13.	
14.	
15.	
16.	
17.	
18.	
19.	
20.	
21.	
22.	
23.	

24.	
25.	

PART THREE – WHAT KIND OF PARENT ARE YOU?

As you take stock of your family life and think about the type of things you might like to improve, this is also a good opportunity to reflect on the type of parent you've become. Without realizing it, the automatic parenting style that's already stored in your subconscious mind is…… the one your parents used with you. And they got their parenting style from their own parents. Of course, it's possible that over the years, it's been refined and got better, but it's useful to stop and check that you haven't accidentally 'inherited' habits that frankly, are not serving you well now.

Read through the parenting styles I've listed below and see if some of these sound and feel familiar. If you recognise bits of yourself here, remember you can put some personal changes for yourself in your Wish List too.

Are you a Firefighting parent? Do you run in to solve battles, deal with emergencies, but never engage with your kids otherwise? Frankly, you're just delighted when things are quiet so you leave well alone. Many of us fall into this trap – 'leave well alone' is a common phrase but your children will learn that they have to play up in order to get your attention.

Are you a Mouse? Do you avoid confrontation and find yourself too afraid to reprimand your kids in public just in case they throw a strop that will cause you all huge embarrassment? Public embarrassment is a horrible feeling that many parents struggle to deal with – by the end of this book, you'll have this problem sorted out.

Are you just plain burnt-out? Exhausted, defeated, you've lost your voice through shouting and there's not an ounce of strength left for yet another round of arguments with the kids, so they pretty much rule the roost. Learning how to take care of yourself, will mean being able to take care of others better.

Or perhaps you're a Lion? The only time you engage with your kids is to tell them off and ROAR! Not only will this make everyone around you feel bad, but it's a quick way of making yourself feel bad too!

Perhaps you're an over-protective parent? You daren't let your kids engage in new activities because you can't trust them not to cause mischief and you're simply not confident enough to deal with potential problems. Rather than avoiding situations all together, it's best to learn how to deal with your own anxiety and avoid passing it on to your children.

Like most parents, you might find yourself switching between these different personas as and when you feel the need arises – perhaps you're a Mouse in the supermarket, a Firefighter during the day and a Lion in the evenings. Be aware that you may just be making things more difficult for yourself for no-one likes dealing with a 'Jekyll and Hyde' type of character. And, laying down strict rules in the heat of the moment, means you'll relax them again when you're feeling tired, have a headache or are simply feeling chilled.

Confused parenting is hard work and my aim is to show you how much easier it can all be, when you're clear about what it is you want.

But for now, you've had time to reflect on some of the challenges in your life and the changes you'd like to make, it's time to find a new way of communicating with your children so you can get things closer to the kind of happy, relaxed, family life you've always wanted.

2) FAMILY CONFERENCE OR MEETING

It may be obvious to say that the most important people who'll be impacted by the changes that you plan to make to the way your family operates, are the members of the family themselves; your children, your partner and anyone else who lives with you. It's going to be important to talk to them about what you are trying to do and why you are doing it.

The best way to introduce new routines and rules is at a Family Conference or Meeting. It doesn't really matter what you decide to call it:

It might be:

- Family conference
- Family meeting
- A meet-up
- Circle time
- Get-together
- Pow-wow
- Encounter
- Rendezvous
- Session

The important thing is that your family get-together becomes a safe, comfortable environment for all family members to discuss and share good news as well as their problems. It's also an opportunity to reflect on what works well around the home and what needs adjusting, with a perhaps a few extra rules and new boundaries thrown in.

And if anyone else has a share of your childcare responsibilities, such as grandparents, nanny, au-pair or neighbour then you can invite them in as a guest from time to time, if you feel the subject being discussed would benefit from their presence.

Gathering for a family conference may feel unnatural at first, but they shouldn't really. Meetings are everywhere. People have them all the time. I've lost count of the number of times I've phoned someone only to be told 'they're in a meeting'. People up and down the country are busy having meetings all the time – breakfast meetings, lunch meetings, strategy meetings, annual meetings, parent-teacher meetings – the list is endless. Go to your local coffee shop, or pub, and it will be full of yet more people meeting. Mums with babies in buggies, friends catching up, people with laptops, the list goes on and on.

Except this rarely seems to happen at home. If anything, we tend to avoid 'meeting' as a family and then we wonder why things don't seem to be running smoothly.

It's always better – and much easier, for that matter, to correct behaviour and introduce changes away from the time when the main source of the problem occurs.

If, for example, the issue is food fussiness, it's not a good idea to engage in arguments midway through the meal. It's much better to gather everyone round, away from the dinner table, at a neutral time of day where you can calmly discuss your ideas with confidence and use pre-suppositions such as: *"And when we start following the new menu ideas that we've come up with today, you'll quickly see how much easier it's going to be to feel happier about sitting at the table and tasting some of those dishes."*

A family conference is also a great way to teach new skills away from the situation where they will be needed. All sorts of life skills can be practiced during your family meeting – holding a knife and fork, tying shoe laces, folding clothes etc. No-one feels particularly picked upon and it can be turned into a game or challenge.

Gathering your family together like this will make it easier for you to make requests. The discussion will bring the family closer together and will put an end to on-going 'nagging'. Although I would certainly avoid using the meetings as an opportunity to be a 'helicopter' parent hovering over your children, checking up on their school work and scrutinizing their every move.

Meetings need to feel as if they're fun, or your children will simply stop wanting to attend and you'll lose a valuable line of communication.

BENEFITS OF A FAMILY MEETING

A family meeting is effective because:

- It offers opportunities to **discuss family values**, in essence what it means to be a part of your particular family. It will help you to develop your 'brand' and a sense of team spirit. Values are principles, standards or qualities that you consider to be worthwhile, important or desirable. They're the reason why you're motivated to do things.

  Our values – often handed down to us from our own parents – become imprinted on our subconscious minds, so they live deep inside us and form part of our beliefs. It's often the case that we only become fully aware of them when we feel they're being violated. Most of the time we might not realise that they're even there and it's often not uncommon to hear people answer 'I'm not sure, I don't think I have any' when they're asked what their values are.

  It's good to get clear on what your family's values are – or what you'd like them to be. This could be with regards to honesty, safety, success, money, possessions, integrity, spirituality and so on – the more clearly defined they are the fewer family conflicts there are more likely to be, for you'll be raising your children to be aware of what you deem to be acceptable and appropriate.

- **Rules and boundaries** can be set. This is the ideal time to clearly state what is and is not acceptable behaviour. Too often we only decide on a boundary when one child has overstepped the mark and then we reprimand them for it, even though we didn't state clearly enough in the first place what constituted acceptable and non-acceptable behaviour. It's not your child's fault if he didn't know the rules.

It's important to be consistent with your rules – problems occur when boundaries are a bit vague or change from day to day, depending on your mood and how busy you are.

It's often the case that divorced parents have a different set of rules in their respective homes. This is fine as children quickly learn that different rules apply in different places. But it's also all the more reason to be very clear on what is and isn't acceptable in your own home.

- It will **reduce sibling rivalry** and jealousy. Any notable individual achievements and successes can be put into the family pot for everyone to bask in the glory. This goes for the achievements of Mum and Dad too. It's good to feel proud of fellow family members and learn how to congratulate others. Children who learn how to do this are more likely to go to be successful themselves.

- It helps your child to **develop communication skills** because they'll learn how to start putting their feelings into words. This includes learning how to apologise to each other and it's good if adults can take the lead on this. Very often children see their parents arguing in front of them, yet never see them apologise or make up, for this is usually done in private. Do it in public and your children will learn to copy you.

- It aids **problem solving**. The group meeting encourages your child to describe a problem they might be having and then think creatively about solutions. Everyone can contribute a suggestion to solve the problem and these can be written down (aim to get at least 10 items on the list) and then the child with the problem can discard the suggestions that don't appeal and think about ways to utilise and implement the solution that does. Your child will also learn that there's nothing wrong with coming up with an idea that, on reflection, turns out not to be a good idea after all. There's no shame, no blame, only praise for making the list of possible solutions even longer. And the most outlandish, wacky idea can get a great big laugh. In fact, I'd recommend that all adults come up with a silly idea that gets thrown out, simply to show that it's not the end of the world to get it wrong and get laughed at.

- **Unwanted behaviours can be corrected** more effectively as you can teach children to recognise their own triggers eg:

"I've noticed that you often feel out of sorts and irritable on long car journeys. Do you think it might be because you feel too hot sitting in your coat? Maybe taking it off in the car next time, might help you to feel better? What do you think? Shall we try that next time?"

Or

"I've noticed that you often feel cross and bothered the night before a test at school. Do you think those feelings of worry are getting on top of you? Would it help if we went through the exercises for an extra 15 minutes each night for the week before?"

Or

"I've noticed that you get upset whenever I ask you to help with clearing the table after dinner. I was wondering what it is about helping to tidy up that you find difficult? Is it stacking the dishwasher? Would it help if I showed you how to do it?"

MY FAMILY CONFERENCE – HOW IT ALL STARTED

I first happened upon the idea of a Family Conference following a complete melt-down in my household, which spoiled something that should have been a pleasant event. Let me explain.

I had spent a long time back and forth on the phone to a travel agent organising a summer holiday for the kids and myself. Finally, after much discussion, he called me up to confirm the details. At the end of the conversation, I put the phone down feeling on top of the world. It was all booked and I could now look forward to a week relaxing in the sun.

"We're going on holiday," I announced, unable to contain my excitement. "It's all booked and we're going to go to Italy to sit on the beach and make sandcastles."

My daughter jumped up in excitement and just at that moment her 7 year-old brother came into the room.

"What's going on?" he asked.

"Mummy said we're going on holiday to Italy to make sandcastles," my daughter said proudly and gave a little dance around the kitchen.

"Why didn't you tell ME?" my son said, his face crumpled with disappointment. "Why did you have to tell HER first without telling ME?"

He stomped off in a stroppy mood, just in time to meet his 10 year-old brother in the corridor.

"What's going on?" he said, after taking one look at his fury.

The 7 year-old told his older brother and, well, you can probably guess the rest. Within moments, the 10 year-old came into the room and started yelling. "Oh, that's terrific. Tell everyone else except ME. How come they both know we're going on holiday and I DON'T!"

At this point, my 5 year-old decided she'd had enough and burst out crying. The 7 year-old came back into the room and decided he couldn't stand the sound of her crying and gave her a great big thump. My daughter howled twenty times louder and so the 10 year-old decided to thump the 7 year-old, just to even things out. So, he started howling too!

Reader, let me tell you, at this point, *I* felt like crying too. All I had done was book a holiday for me and the kids. It was supposed to be a nice thing to do; a special treat.

The last thing in the world I wanted right then was a holiday away with my children. How on earth would I survive a week in their company with that kind of behaviour?

Later that evening, I sat down and had a long, hard think about the day's events.

My ex-husband and I had separated 18-months earlier and whilst we had all got used to the new living arrangements, I realised that anxiety was underpinning the children's extreme reaction. The foundations of their family life had been shaken up and whilst on the surface, we were all coping well, it only took one 'out of the ordinary' event (even if it was a nice one like a holiday) to be mentioned for them to start feeling well and truly rattled.

I realised it had been unfair of me to spring the news of the holiday on them like that and vowed never to do that again.

Our 'Family Conference' was born. The next day, I sat them round the kitchen table and started the 'holiday' story all over again. From then on, I only ever shared 'news' when we were all together as a group.

It clearly left a good lasting impression, for any time after that whenever I mentioned having a Family Conference, they'd get really excited and eagerly run to the kitchen table. I think they thought I was going to tell them that we were going on holiday again!

Your Family Conference doesn't even have to take place formally around a table, although it's useful to have a table to sit round to call people's attention to the meeting. It is also easier if you want to write things down on paper or in a notebook or even on your laptop or tablet.

But it could also be:

- Sitting in a circle on a rug on the living room floor.
- On a blanket in the garden.
- As part of a picnic in the park.
- On a bed surrounded by comfy cushions.
- Late in the evening, creating a camp fire (if you have a safe place) and cooking sausages.
- On a night time walk by torchlight.

In fact, I would recommend that you pick a different or more unusual location now and again, especially if you find your meetings not going as well as you'd like them to or your children not receptive to the idea of new rules and boundaries.

Don't stick to the same seating plan every time either. It's good to shuffle places and you might find your children are more creative and relaxed in a different seat.

If you have a new idea you want to present to the kids that you'll be looking for group approval, with everyone 'on message', it's a good idea to seat your family 'theatre style' with everyone looking in the same direction. Remember: as we think, speak and hear words spoken, our minds are making images in front of us. With everyone facing the same direction, you'll be able to point to the space in front as you describe your idea. If everyone is looking the same way, they'll start to see the same things and you're more likely to get their approval.

Likewise, if a situation has come up that requires a bit of family brainstorming, you're better off seating everyone around a table.

Sitting on opposite sides will give them different perspectives and you're more likely to get a variety of ideas.

Always take time after the meeting to reflect: how well did things go? What worked well and what didn't? What could you do better next time – and how?

T I P : Do remember to include good news. In fact, I'd recommend starting the meeting by going around the group and asking for good or funny news. It will set the tone for the meeting and your children will see it as an enjoyable practice.

HOW TO GET KIDS TALKING

It's all good and well planning a get together meeting for the family, but what happens if your kids just aren't 'talkers'. Or if one of them dominates the conversation and you find the others are happy to stay quiet.

If you're starting your get-togethers with young children, it's very likely that you won't have too many problems in getting them to contribute. But if you're introducing these meetings for the first time to older children or teenagers, there may be an element of distrust on their part and a reluctance to participate. Follow these tips:

Remember to use open questions (see Words that Work section) start sentences with words like *What, Why, Where, How* rather than *Did you…*

Ask for more details:

- *And what was the best bit about that?*
- *Then what happened?*
- *I'm intrigued, what happened next?*
- *So, tell me more…*

Make observations:

- *You looked like you really enjoyed that*
- *I can see that you put extra effort in doing that well*
- *That's interesting*

Give 100% attention: We get cross with our kids if we're talking to them and they don't seem to be listening. It's a horrible feeling and we end up wondering if there's any point in continuing. Your child feels exactly the same. If they're talking to you, you must give them your full attention and look at them. That means no checking your phone, writing things in a notepad, picking your fingernails, feeding the cat, emptying the washing machine etc. etc. Ignore this advice and, one day, you'll find that they will simply give up and stop talking to you all together.

Be a good listener: Yes, it can get frustrating listening to a child who's taking forever to tell a story, but don't be tempted to jump in and finish off their sentences to speed things up. Use prompts such as: *ah ha, I see, oh OK, mmm* to keep the flow going.

You don't have to solve every problem: Have you ever told a friend about a problem you've been experiencing, only to have them interrupt every few sentences by offering a solution? Annoying isn't it? Often the advice they give is inappropriate and if only they would listen to the end of the story, they'd know and understand that! It's the same for your child. Sometimes they just need to get something off their chest to feel better. So if you're hearing that they were pushed over at school, a simple *Oh, that's not nice – were you hurt anywhere?* may be enough. As much as you may want to rush into school to tell the other child off and report it to the teachers, your child isn't asking you to do that. He just wants a sympathetic ear and probably a hug.

Aim to have Family Conferences little and often when it involves young children. You can keep the meetings to a short 15 or 20 minutes and have them once or even twice a week. Older children and teenagers might start feeling a little 'under the spotlight' if these meetings are too frequent, so once every two weeks is probably better. If you start having them as little as once a month, I suspect you'll lose the feeling of continuity and a sense of 'oh, what am I going to get told off about now' will start to creep in.

Exercise – Three Chairs

Not every family squabble or disagreement will be resolved simply by talking it through. In fact, there'll be occasions when it could make things worse. If you or a family member is struggling to see the other person's point of view, consider using this NLP exercise:

This is an exercise in reflection for you to do on your own. You will need three chairs, about four feet away from each other, set out in a triangle. Focus on a situation you encountered recently with a family member where you both had different perspectives and struggled to reach an agreement.

1st position: Sit in the first chair and experience that situation once more, through your own perspective. What are you thinking, feeling, hearing and saying to yourself as you look across to the second chair, which represents the other person? Take a few moments to recall all your feelings and say them out loud. You can be honest; say exactly what you'd like to say. Sit here for a few minutes until you're sure you've covered all your feelings.

2nd position: Now move to the second chair and pretend to be the other person. What experience are you having now? What are you thinking and feeling as you look across to the 'person' (ie. you) in the first chair? Again, speak out loud as if you really were this person and say what you believe that person would be thinking. Take your time to do this.

3rd position: Now move across to the third chair and take a few moments to observe both 'people' in the other chairs. Think about how these two people have related to each other and to the situation. Take a look at the first chair and ask yourself what advice you could give.

If you still need greater insight, repeat this exercise by sitting in each of the chairs again. Notice how you might feel differently about the original situation.

Once you've got the hang of the process, carry out this exercise with other family members especially siblings to resolve their differences.

3) PRAISE AND REWARDS

I'm often asked if it's a good idea to introduce rewards as an additional incentive to get children to behave well and this is a good place in the book to address this thorny issue. After all, if you are going to expect big changes in behaviour you might be tempted to 'help' things along a little by offering something by way of a tangible pat on the back.

On the face of it, some sort of recognition in the form of a coveted item, does sound like a good idea. We're all naturally goal-seeking individuals and surely if anyone is expected to push themselves in order to achieve something, then offering a carrot may well make all the difference to their level of motivation.

Rewards have become a modern parenting phenomenon and in recent years there has been a real noticeable trend to give children money or gifts in exchange for just about anything from good exam results at school to simply being 'good'.

Some families employ elaborate charts and league tables, showering their prodigy with gold stars for brushing their teeth, being quiet in the back of the car or simply refraining from arguing with siblings for an hour or two. Ten gold stars equals a new toy.

Rewarding and praising children – rather than punishing and disciplining – has grown in popularity to such a degree that few of us stop to question whether it's actually a good idea. Most people do it simply because it just 'feels' like good parenting.

If you are the type of parent that has doggedly stuck to a rewards system in the hope of changing your child's behaviour you may be unwilling to change tactic now, particularly when the changes being discussed here seem so huge they may well require some enticement. However, you might like to think again. Studies of this modern trend are now beginning to show that when children expect or anticipate rewards, they can actually end up performing *more* poorly. They get into the routine of doing things simply to impress. In doing so they become very reliant on 'outside opinion' rather than developing a good sense of who and what they are.

A well-known experiment carried out in 1975 by the psychologist Edward L. Deci and colleagues featured two groups of students who were invited to work on an interesting puzzle. One half of the group was paid to do this and for the other half there was no reward involved.

It was discovered that the group who received no payment ended up being significantly more keen to continue to play with the puzzle in their free time. It was also reported that they showed more enthusiasm for the task and were able to engage with it more and as a result were more successful. The other group's eye was clearly looking in the direction of the financial reward and as a result they did all that was asked of them and no more.

Many experiments have been carried out since, with variations in the task assigned and the reward offered. In each case, the results have been replicated, with the conclusion that more pleasure and success can be derived from a task if there's no distracting element such as a reward.

Of course, there has to be something positive to be gained out of any kind of task, otherwise there would be no point doing it. But keeping your end goal in sight as your 'reward' is going to increase your chances of getting there.

Look at this another way. Consider all the tasks that we do that are not necessarily pleasurable but essential eg: washing the car; cooking the family supper; weeding the garden; clearing out a cupboard; polishing shoes. These are tasks that all need doing from time to time and are not particularly pleasurable. For most of us the reward lies in the reaction to what we've done, say when the family happily tucks in to the Sunday roast, or the benefit we feel from having neatly organised cupboards.

That's our reward – and it feels good. Likewise, when we've weeded the garden or washed the family car the satisfaction comes when we stand back and take a look at our handiwork. I can't be the only person who's gone back an hour after completing a job to take a sneaky peek at how clean and tidy it all is, just to get another 'feel good injection'.

Each time you dangle rewards and bribes under your child's nose in order to get them to finish their homework, or tidy their bedroom, you're diluting the effect of that 'feel good injection'. You're literally sucking the life out of life!

That doesn't mean that your child will never get a treat again – but a treat is not the same as an enticement. So, having a day trip out to a theme park to celebrate the end of the school year and the hard work put in to get through exams, is a great idea.

But it's not the same as saying "if you work hard and get good grades, then I will take you out to the theme park". Because after all, what's going to happen if your child doesn't get good grades? And how hard does he need to work to satisfy you? Are you going to cancel the trip to the theme park? That's really not going to make anyone feel good and it's simply not enjoyable parenting.

I was always of the opinion that if any of my children got bad grades at school, they were probably *more* in need of a day trip out to let off steam, not less. And once you start 'rewarding' it follows that you have to start 'unrewarding' too, so you'll be missing out on opportunities to give your child exactly what they need, when they need it.

Encourage children to think about what will happen as a result of doing the task eg: *"That's three nights in a row you've organised your school things for the next day. It's getting easier to arrive earlier and meet your friends in the playground for a game of football before school starts, isn't it?"*

And just to clear up any confusion, keeping a chart on the bedroom wall with a checklist for things that need doing is fine. These can be ticked off in the usual way – that's teaching your child to be focused and organised. Rather than sticking a star on the chart, you could encourage your child to fill in some extra details, say for example, how long the activity took and what could be done to improve or make things run more smoothly the next day.

That way, if your child hasn't tidied the bedroom particularly well, rather than not handing out the usual shiny star (which is never a good thing to be doing just before bed time!), he can make a note that he'll need to start tidying 10 minutes earlier the next day, or get some extra storage boxes as the ones he has are now too small.

Likewise keeping a Success Journal or Diary to track progress is a very good idea – for studies have shown that what gets measured, automatically improves. It's why I've included a Journal at the end of this book. I know that this will help you on your way and you're more likely to be successful in making changes to your parenting style if you use it. It may seem strange but you'd be less successful if someone offered you a luxury holiday for doing so. Sure, it would be lovely to have a holiday once you've sorted the sibling squabbles, fussy eating, exam stress – you'll deserve one for sure, but dreaming of white sandy beaches, cocktails on the terrace and a bit of water-skiing is not going to help you with the task in hand. Noticing what's working well and what needs changing is the best way forward for you.

Aside from the damaging and diluting effects of the modern tendency to over-reward, it is worth remembering there is a rather more unpalatable aspect of rewarding children's compliance. It reduces the relationship between the two parties to 'controller' and 'controlled'. It might work well with a young child but it's not a surprise that teenagers start to rebel against it and make demands for ever more expensive items. They're doing what teenagers are supposed to do – separate from their parents and become autonomous beings. All you'll be doing is adding friction into the relationship and keeping them small.

At the end of the day, you'll want to raise self-motivated and intrinsically happy children, rather than reward-addicts and people-pleasers. It is not only better for them, but also makes parenting a whole lot easier! To pick up ideas on how to encourage children without resorting to bribery, remember to refer back to the 'Words that Work' Chapter at the beginning.

GIVING YOUR CHILD A FEEDBACK SANDWICH

Your child won't get everything right first time and it is well worth planning strategies now for how you'll deal with the fact that, from time to time, you'll need to give some negative feedback and a nudge in the right direction. How you deliver this feedback will make all the difference. I recommend using the feedback sandwich, which consists of one specific criticism sandwiched between specific praises.

To demonstrate the feedback sandwich, I am going to use the example of a child who repeatedly spills drinks over the table.

1. **Prepare:** Don't dive in without thinking through what you're going to say. It's easy to get frustrated and lose control but this will only throw you off balance and ruin all your good work. It is possible this problem might occur again, even probable, but be ready for it and calm in your response.

2. **Identify the positive:** Find something good to say. For example: *"I really appreciate you helping so enthusiastically, to lay the table in the evenings."* And as you're doing this, look your child in the eye and smile – your child is receiving praise.

3. **Present the facts:** Follow on by mentioning the problem: *"I've noticed that it can be tricky to pour the drinks though and sometimes the tablecloth gets wet."* As you're doing this, look away from your child so that they don't take the negative impact of your comments as a personal criticism. That's why it's good to have a notebook in front of you to look at.

   The example that I'm giving you is quite trivial but imagine for a moment that you were giving feedback about pre-discussed homework routines being broken or an agreed time for coming home after Saturday night's party not being adhered to. It would be useful to point to the notes from a previous meeting where agreement had been reached. It's easier to avoid your child's gaze if you're doing something like this – after all, it's the behaviour that you're unhappy with and not your child. Teenagers can often feel 'picked on' without their parents doing anything at all, so this will help minimize those feelings too.

4. **Present the solution:** *"So I thought it would be a good idea for us to work together on this – I can show you how to pour the drinks without spilling a drop. There's a special way of doing it to keep the table dry – I'll show you and you can practise."* And if you're not sure of the solution immediately, you can say something like *"Let's take a few moments to think about what might be the best thing to do in this situation."*

5. **Give a bright outlook:** Keep your language positive and take the conversation forwards. Say: *"I enjoy it when we do things together and we'll get the table looking really smart, won't we?'*

6. **Follow-up in the future:** Remind the child of the good work they've done and the progress they've made by referring back to

it in a positive way later on. You can use it to keep motivation levels up: *"I know it can be tricky to tie your own shoelaces at first but these things get easier with time. Do you remember how you used to struggle to pour the drinks at supper time? We were forever having those sopping, wet tablecloths! And then, with a little bit of practice you figured it out and now you can pour the drinks really easily. Can't you?"*

Think about examples from your own family experience and plot out your own feedback sandwich for future use. You'll quickly discover it is a useful pattern to follow whenever you need to point out something that's not working well at the moment.

4) THE 80 / 20 RULE

Another technique that will make a huge difference to your peace of mind is based on the well-known 80/20 rule.

Whatever your current style of parenting, be it fire-fighting parent, lion or mouse, you'll know how exhausting that can be. Each time there's a flare-up, you'll do your utmost to attempt to sort it out. Some days you'll be feeling as if this is all that you do: sort out emergencies.

It's no surprise then that most parents tend to keep a low profile when things are going well. They don't want to upset the apple cart and see things kick off again. Unfortunately, this lack of on-going engagement is precisely what encourages children to play up time and again. It's a vicious circle.

Ironically though, what most people don't realise is that most of the things that they've been worrying about and attempting to sort out, are actually going to make very little difference to the smooth running of the household. Not only were the constant battles ineffective and exhausting, they were ones you never needed to fight.

For this final section of preparation, let me introduce you to The 80/20 Rule.

You may be familiar with the Pareto Principle (also known as the 80/20 rule). It states that, for many events, roughly 80 per cent of the effects come from 20 per cent of the causes. The principle is named after an Italian economist Vilfredo Pareto, who observed in 1906 that around 80 per cent of the land in Italy was owned by 20 per cent of the population, or thereabouts. He went on to develop his principle after observing that 20 per cent of the pea pods in his garden contained 80 per cent of the peas. And vice versa – 80 per cent of the pods only held 20 per cent of the peas.

It has now become a common rule of thumb in the business world. For example, 80 per cent of sales come from 20 per cent of a company's clients. It has also been found to work well when applied to pretty much all areas of our lives.

Using this principle, we can deduce that 80 per cent of your frustration around the home is being wasted. Shocked? Let's look at some facts:

- **The shoes in your wardrobe:** 80 per cent of the shoes in your wardrobe rarely get worn – so that's the sparkly, strappy sandals, the outrageously high slingbacks, the beige suede boots and the black ones for that matter, the night-club ones, the holiday flip-flops......

  20 per cent of the shoes get worn frequently – yup, that's the boring black ones, the trainers and wellies (if you have a dog, as I do).

- **Your household income:** 80 per cent of your income goes on 20 per cent of your household expenditure – gosh, that's a sad statistic but if you add up your energy bills and mortgage, it's probably about right.

20 per cent of your income has to stretch across the other 80 per cent of things you spend your money on, such as food, clothes, car, hairdressing, holidays, dentist, going out.

- **Your telephone contact list:** 80 per cent of the people on your telephone contact list you only speak to 20 per cent of the time. I'm sure most of us would be delighted to delete most of our contact list nowadays – do we even know them all?

  20 per cent of contacts, you'll be on the phone to 80 per cent of the time. And just one person might take up the bulk of that time!

- **Family mealtimes:** 80 per cent of the time you eat pretty much the same meals in rotation ie. 20 per cent of your repertoire. So that's spag bol, roast chicken, pizza... am I right?

  20 per cent of the time you might be a bit more adventurous and dip into the 80 per cent of other recipes you know, but rarely use.

- **Social media platforms:** This pattern is even replicated on social media platforms – on Twitter a few people are responsible for most of the tweets, again around 20/80. The official figures released are that just 10 per cent of the people produce 60 per cent of the tweets.

So, what does this have to do with helping you manage your child's behaviour? Well, rather a lot actually.

Do you remember the Wish List I asked you to create at the beginning of this section? Hopefully you were able to put some thought into it and came up with a nice long list of all the things that really annoy you or quite obviously need changing. I deliberately encouraged you to think about all the little things you'd like to change. Some of the things you noted down might have been pretty small, but they create a little niggle in our minds and drag us down.

But here's the thing:

Applying the Pareto Principle we can deduce that '*80 per cent of the items on your list will only make a 20 per cent difference or improvement to your life*'.

Let's think about that again.

'80 per cent of the things on your list' – so that's most of them, right? – will only make 'a 20 per cent difference or improvement' – that's not much, is it? I don't know about you, but I'd like more than that for my efforts.

BUT, if the principle works then that also means that *20 per cent* of the things on your list will make an *80 per cent* overall difference to your family life right now.

Hey, that sounds much better, doesn't it? Hands up all those who want an 80 *per cent* improvement.........

I'm interested in that special 20 per cent that will make all the difference to the smooth running and happiness of your home – and you should be too. All you need to do is focus on these problems and only these problems to start with. It doesn't mean that you'll forget about all the other things forever. It is just that right now, you'll put them to one side.

So, what's the next step? It is quite simple:

I'd like you to refer back to your Wish List and count up the number of items on it.

Then divide the total by 5. What number do you get?

Eg: 32 items divided by 5 = 6.4

If this is your calculation, use this number as your guide and now pick the SIX most important things on that Wish List. Ask yourself the question: if I could only choose six items, which ones would I choose first?

These are your goals for the moment. Because, fixing these six things will make an 80 per cent improvement to the happiness of the home. Don't get distracted by the other things that are still on your list. Remember: everything is possible. It's just not possible to do everything right now. The more things you try to tackle at the same time, the less chance there is of you becoming successful. This lack of success at managing your children's behaviour will gnaw away at your self-confidence, send out the wrong message to both them and to yourself – and lessen your chances for any kind of future success.

In fact, delete 80 per cent of your list right now. These are things that you won't forget. By doing this you'll simply put them out of your mind until you revisit them some time in the future. As soon as you start to achieve some of your goals, you'll be able to cross them off your list and free up space for other items.

OK, so I'll admit now that some of these items may never get revisited. As parents it's something that we have to learn to live with – nothing will ever be perfect and the chances are your children will grow up, leave home and you'll still have a few items on your list that never got sorted out. I know I certainly have a few! And from time to time, I have to remind myself that the reason these things never got sorted out, is because we were all busy doing other things.

Go back now to your original Wish List and divide the total number of items by five. This is the 20 per cent that will make an 80 per cent improvement to your lives. And in the next section, I'll be showing you how to structure those 'wishes' and change them into goals with well-formed outcomes, so you'll be able to achieve them more easily.

5) TURNING YOUR WISHES INTO GOALS

Most of us are used to setting goals and targets for ourselves in the form of New Year's resolutions. Think back to some of the ones you've set for yourself in the past and become aware of your successes and then, also your failures.

Like most people, you can probably count the successes on the fingers of one hand, whilst being able to make a long, long list of all those you failed to achieve. But it's not surprising that most of us do fail to stick resolutions, for they're often made on the spur of the moment at midnight, fuelled by alcohol. We often hear that 'resolutions don't work' but in fact we are the problem and not the resolutions – we fail to plan and get a proper goal in place for ourselves.

Well, I'm going to give you a bit of inside knowledge here by telling you about the most common reasons for failing. Read through them and you'll be able to avoid falling into the same trap.

REASONS PEOPLE FAIL TO ACHIEVE THEIR GOALS

Mistake No. 1 – They forget what their goal is.

Yes, seriously, it's as simple as that. Test yourself if you don't believe me. Can you really remember all the New Year resolutions you made last year? And not only the 'lose weight/get fit/quit smoking' ones you told your family about but also those quiet, private ones you made to yourself. What did you tell yourself, honestly?

And have you ever made a commitment to lose weight by stopping eating biscuits let's say, only to find yourself arriving home tired one day, automatically reaching for the biscuit tin. It's only when the digestive is being firmly crunched between your teeth do you utter the words "Oh, I forgot".

Forgetting is what we do well and if you're keen to make changes, you'll need to start remembering what it is you're aiming for. That's why I've included the 21 Day Success Journal for you at the end of this book. It's important to use it so you can remember more easily – take the time to write everything down.

Mistake No. 2 – They focus on what they don't want.

We learnt all about this common mistake in the 'Words that Work' section. Remember to state your goal in the positive and not the negative so – 'I can't stand noisy, messy mealtimes' becomes 'I'd like mealtimes to be calmer and tidier'.

Most of us find it easier to identify what we don't like about our lives, rather than focusing on what we do want – and remember, it matters a great deal. As we think and speak, our minds make mini pictures out of the words we use and almost as if we're operating on auto-pilot, we'll find ourselves being magnetically drawn to those negative pictures – i.e. precisely what we don't want in our lives, rather than what we do. Always phrase your goals in the 'positive' for a positive outcome.

Mistake No. 3 – The goal is far too vague.

Let's take the example that I gave you in Mistake 2. 'I'd like mealtimes to be calmer and tidier' is good because it's framed in the positive but it's still too vague. What specifically will make it calmer and who needs to be making the changes?

Mistake No. 4 – People fail to consider the HOW part.

Having established what they'd like to achieve, most people fail to think about the kind of resources they'll need to achieve their goal. Identify all the resources you'll need in advance – what will you need to get you started and what will you need further down the line? Will you need someone else to help you and will you need to brief them?

Mistake No. 5 – Self-sabotage.

Many of us self-sabotage our goals, because we suddenly find that we don't truly want to achieve them. Quite simply, we made the wrong choice and this is especially true for New Year resolutions that are made on the spur of the moment. Take the time to consider the goals that you've set for yourself and your family – will a successful outcome actually fit in with your life and personal values? Think carefully about how achieving this particular goal will impact others around you.

WRITING YOUR SUCCESS PLAN

So let's get to work by answering each of these questions to clarify your goals. Write down your answers and use them to create a clear and precise Success Plan.

1. Is your goal stated in positive terms? *"I want to have the kids ready for bed earlier"*, rather than *"I don't want bedtimes to drag on half the night"*.

2. Is your goal clearly defined? Be very specific about what it is you're aiming for. So, *"I want to have the kids ready in bed with lights out at 7.30pm"*. Next, think about how you'll achieve this – when, where, how, who? What needs to change in order for you to have any chance at all of achieving this? Will you need to have bath-time earlier and supper-time too, perhaps? Does one child's behaviour need to change in order for your routine to run more smoothly? Will you need help from anyone else to achieve it?

3. Write down a description of how your life will look once you have achieved your goal. It's good to have sensory-based evidence for this – what will you see, feel and hear when you have achieved it? Eg: *"When the kids get into bed earlier and the lights are off at 7.30pm, the house will become peaceful and quiet. I'll be able to cook an evening meal for myself and my partner – the kitchen will be filled with delicious smells and we'll smile at each other as we relax with a glass of wine."* OR *"I'll be able to attend the weekly Yoga class with my friend and feel fitter and healthier as a result. We'll go for a drink afterwards and laugh as we catch up on the week's news."* The more information you can supply, the more you'll know that you've achieved your goal. Imagine yourself at a time in the future when you have achieved all that you want to achieve. Write it down clearly.

4. Does the outcome fit in with your life and personal values? Is it meaningful for you? Think carefully about how your goal will impact others around you. Would you really want the kids in bed sleeping by 7.30pm if you or your partner work long hours and don't see much of the children? Asking yourself questions like 'When don't I want this outcome?' will enable you to set appropriate boundaries for yourself.

5. Have you identified the resources you'll need? What will you need to get you started – will you need someone else's help? And will anything else need to change? If you want to get the kids into bed by 7.30pm how will you manage it on Tuesdays when one goes to after-school swimming and the other has piano lessons? Will sharing the pick-ups with another parent to speed up the process of getting everyone back home, be possible? Could the children's evening meal be prepared the night before, so it's all ready to eat when you come home? And what will you need further down the line? Have you ever managed this before? Would you benefit from getting advice from someone who has done this before? Is there more than one way to achieve this outcome? Which way will be best for you?

6. What's your first step going to be? And then the next? Having ensured that your goal or outcome is now 'well-formed', you'll need to clearly define that first step into action. What will it be? If your goal or target feels enormous and almost out of reach, break it down into smaller steps. Your first step needs to be manageable because if you do not take it, you will not take any of the others either. Perhaps your first step will be picking up the telephone and asking someone for advice. What will the next steps be?

Here are a couple of examples of how you could think about your goals in their entirety. You'll see that I always start with a precise date – it's good to set a time frame as this will help you to achieve it.

"It is 25th September and the children have been back at school for 3 weeks. Having discussed a new routine with them during one of our regular Family Meetings, evenings are more organised. After a brief snack in the kitchen once they are home from school, homework is now completed in the dining room. Having the kitchen to myself means I can be more focused and cook tasty suppers more easily. We now eat half an hour earlier than we used to and the children are in bed with lights out at 7.30pm. My partner tells me he appreciates our evening time together."

"It is 24th February and Josh and Freddie are getting along much better now. Having installed new shelving and cupboards in the bedroom, each has a separate area to call their own. The room is much tidier now and it's easier to store things and find them again quickly when we need them. The arguments have stopped and they both enjoy having one-to-one time with a bedtime story in their own special corner."

Remember, to get to this point you'll have to break each one down into the small steps you'll need to be taking to get there. But having this 'big picture' in your mind, will be the 'reward' that will spur you on to keep going till you get there.

12

Get Into The Right State

Just to make one thing clear before we go any further, this chapter is all about getting yourself into 'THE' right state, rather than 'A' right state. Most of you are probably familiar with the feelings that come with being 'in a right state', for when your kids are driving you up the wall, few of us look at our best.

Communication is made up of much more than simply words and studies show that our body language accounts for around 50%. Most of us have experienced situations of being in conversation with someone whose 'inside' doesn't match their 'outside'. A good example of this would be a sales assistant in a shop – have you ever had to complain and return goods? The assistant may have listened to your concerns whilst smiling politely on the outside, but their true feelings of annoyance were also written all over their face.

It's not easy to hoodwink children and in fact, because their senses are at the developmental stage they are much more likely to pick up on all the other signals that you're sending out – quite literally, they're more 'sensitive'. The same can happen with family pets – if you own a dog, you'll know that your pet can sense when all is not well without you having to say a word.

That's why I'd like you to think about getting yourself into THE right state before rushing headlong into changing your family routines and setting new boundaries. You may get away with saying the 'magic words' through gritted teeth, but that will only take you so far. I want to make sure you can be as successful as you possibly can be.

If you're tired and stressed, your family will suffer. We start operating on our auto-pilot, using the parenting that's been programmed into our subconscious minds by our own parents. Even if it wasn't too bad, it's probably outdated and no longer an appropriate way to raise today's modern child. Stressed parents can dent their child's confidence without realising it and your child will quickly learn that they're never 'good enough' for you.

When you're energized and motivated, your family benefits and the point of this chapter is to help you feel mentally and physically prepared. After all, no-one would consider entering for a Marathon without several months of training and yet raising a family is a marathon task that many of us are ill-prepared for. Unlike a Marathon race though, we can't come back again next year and run the race again, hoping for a better outcome. We only get one shot at parenting our children.

SELF-CARE

So, how do you know when you're a stressed out parent who's reached their limit and had enough? What is it about your behaviour that would indicate this? Is it:

- Shouting and getting angry?
- Confiscating favourite toys and sending kids to their bedrooms?
- Needing an extra glass of wine at night, or two even?
- A bar of chocolate to cheer yourself up?
- Forever feeling emotional and crying?

If any of those signs start creeping into your life, then you've allowed your stress levels to build up and spill over. It's far better to nip things in the bud by creating an 'early warning system' for yourself.

Creating an early warning system will enable you to recognise when it's time to take action. Read the following list of symptoms and mark the ones that you tend to experience most when you are under stress.

Select **three** of the most common symptoms from each category. These can then be used as your own early warning system.

And if you can think of any other symptoms that aren't on the list, then do add these in too.

Physical symptoms

- Indigestion
- Stomach cramps
- Constipation or diarrhoea
- Shoulder, neck and back pain
- Persistent headaches
- Chronic sinus problems
- Humming in the ears
- Frequent viral infections
- Weight loss or gain
- Frequent urination
- Skin problems
- Tired eyes and visual disturbances
- Stiffness

- Frequent 'pins and needles'
- Attacks of dizziness
- Rapid shallow breathing and palpitations

Emotional symptoms

- An increase in anxiety and fearfulness
- Becoming easily hurt and upset
- Being tearful
- Feeling irritable
- Having a sense of worthlessness and apathy
- Lacking confidence
- Being confused or overwhelmed
- Being humourless
- Getting over-excited

Behavioural symptoms

- Poor concentration
- An inability to listen well
- Forgetfulness
- Restlessness
- Talking too much
- Nervous habits such as biting nails
- Inability to make decisions and sort priorities
- Poor planning
- Reluctance to delegate
- 'Making mountains out of molehills'
- An increase in phobic fears and obsessions
- Increased consumption of alcohol, nicotine etc
- Insomnia and nightmares
- Impotence and loss of libido
- Unkempt appearance and untidiness
- Loss of control over finances
- Over-protectiveness and over-cautiousness

You should be able to spot the physical and emotional signs yourself, but you may not be so aware of the behavioural ones, so you may need to ask another family member to help you monitor these – and they might like to create a list for themselves too.

So, once you've chosen the **three** most common symptoms that you experience from each category, write them down here:

Physical	Emotional	Behavioural

1.

2.

3.

This is now your 'early warning system'. Make a promise to yourself that if four or more of these symptoms start to trouble you, you'll take action to nip them in the bud.

If you're anything like I was when my children were young, you'll probably be able to tick off most of those symptoms and put it down to being a parent. It goes with the territory, doesn't it? For a few years, I accepted that this was how my life was going to be simply because I had young children to look after.

But it doesn't need to be like that. Make a promise to yourself that you'll start taking better care of yourself. Not only will you feel better, but your children will feel better too and life around the home will become easier and happier for you all.

Make a list of all the different types of action you could take to help detox the stress out of your life. These are just a few of my suggestions and you can add to them:

Internal Dialogue: We've talked a lot about the use of words and language in this book, but what about your own internal dialogue? What kind of words are you using when you speak to yourself? Do you wind yourself up over small irritating matters until they make you boiling mad? Do you re-run past failures and disappointments? Do you have an "It's not fair" kind of conversation going on? All of this will be having a negative effect on your mood and emotional state, so remember to edit not only the words that come out of your mouth but also the ones inside your head.

Diet: Lots of foods alter our stress and anxiety levels as well as create mood swings. When you're feeling stressed and sleep-deprived your body will start craving exactly the kind of foods it's best to avoid at this time – you know the ones I mean, for I've mentioned them many times in this book already: sugary treats, white bread, pasta, cheese, take-away meals. Don't kid yourself that you 'need' these at this time. Foods to eat plenty of include: porridge, boiled potatoes, brown rice, wholegrain breads, fish, turkey, chicken, cottage cheese, avocados, beans, plenty of fruit and vegetables in general. There's no need to starve yourself, in fact you shouldn't, but fill up on energy foods.

Avoid toxins: Reduce caffeine levels eg. coffee, tea, chocolate, coffee-flavoured ice-cream and cakes. If you struggle to sleep at night be aware of the stimulating effects of cheese, red meat, alcohol and nicotine. It's also wise to reduce salt intake.

Exercise: The higher our physical tension levels, the more likely it is that we will experience bouts of anxiety and feelings of frustration and anger. Regular exercise (at least 20 minutes each day) such as walking, will use up excess adrenaline and release endorphins. Aim to take your exercise outdoors in a nearby park or open space for this will be better than cooped up, sweating away in an airless gym.

Learn breathing and relaxation techniques: You'll find many ideas for these throughout this book, for I believe they're really important – they're easy to learn and you'll feel the benefits almost immediately.

Stimulate your senses: Burning aromatherapy candles or exciting your taste buds with new and different types of foods will light up parts of the brain that your day-to-day life may not. You'll be giving the 'over-used' parts a well-earned break. Consider having a massage for example and avoid the cinema if you spend your day in front of a computer screen.

Laughter: Laughing in response to day-to-day problems may not be an obvious choice for most of us, but experts are agreed that it may be the best medicine and the quickest way to change your brain chemistry. Watch funny movies, TV programmes or listen to comedy on the radio on a regular basis.

Get up earlier: I can already hear the cries of "NO, I can't possibly get up any earlier" and I'll admit that when we're feeling exhausted it's often the last thing we want to be doing. Unless you have a baby that still requires feeding at night, I'd recommend you grit your teeth and set your alarm for 30 minutes earlier. You'll feel more in control, the day will run more smoothly and you'll feel more relaxed as a result. And you'll fall asleep easier at night too, rather than tossing and turning with worry.

Avoid criticism: Don't talk about your kids in a critical way to other people. If you're repeatedly telling others that your children are unruly, noisy, untidy, lazy, can't be bothered with school work and never listen to you, you'll be sending yourself subtle hypnotic messages that you're a really lousy parent. Over time you'll begin to believe it more and it will erode your own self-confidence.

Take a photo: A happy one of you and your kids smiling and laughing. Stick it on the fridge or keep it on your phone. Look at it several times a day and show it to your children regularly too. The more you look at this picture, the more your 'self-image' of how you are as a family will change from negative to positive.

As I said, these are just a few examples and you can be creative and come up with your own ideas.

I remember back to a particularly stressful time in my life when I was going through my divorce. My children were still young – ages 4, 6 and 9 years – and they were at different schools with timetables that forever clashed so I was always in the car frantically driving back and forth. I was still running my Montessori School and it needed setting up from scratch (including furniture) really early in the morning – I sometimes went there at the crack of dawn before breakfast and took the children with me. This kind of scenario went on for a couple of years – not only was it exhausting but I remember feeling constantly worried and anxious. I spent my life running everywhere and got very thin (every cloud…).

I knew I had to somehow get more time in the day if we were to get through this and actually enjoy life too (let's not forget that) so I had to start thinking of different ways to achieve this. First of all, I decided to create a monochrome wardrobe for myself – I could never find anything to wear in the morning that reasonably matched and invariably the ironing wasn't up-to-date. This was eating into valuable, precious minutes. So, I made a decision to only ever wear black – that way, on dark mornings I knew that whatever I pulled out of the wardrobe would go with whatever else I was wearing. It might sound a little sombre but by sticking to a single colour, I found myself becoming very much more appreciative of the styles, design, textures and fabrics of clothes. And in the summer time, ankle length long flowing black skirts are actually very cooling.

Next, I stopped blow-drying and styling my hair – from now on I pinned it up casually on top of my head. And I only wore flat shoes – too much running, see. Then I cut out alcohol completely and got really into eating uber-healthy foods that would give me more energy.

And finally, I stopped cleaning the house. I figured it was more important to have the time to sit and read books to my children than worry about dust in the corners. I made the decision to only clean bathrooms and the kitchen and so long as the house was tidy and organised (this was important to me) and the children had clean clothes and were well fed, then it really wouldn't matter about anything else.

I didn't vacuum or dust anywhere in the house for eight weeks – and somehow it made us all feel so much more relaxed. The dirt stopped showing after a while and the dust collected in little puff balls on the stairs. Each time we walked up and down stairs they would rise a little and then bounce down to sit on a different stair. The children started 'playing' with them, giving them a poke and a prod to watch them float up in the air – and I'm sure my daughter cried when I did eventually get around to vacuuming them away.

Be creative.

Start thinking of ideas right now where you can save yourself precious minutes – for these minutes will add up to an extra chunk of time. Extra time to sit and hug your children, feeling relaxed and close, extra time to read books, paint pictures together and go for walks. Remember – one day they'll be grown-up and gone.

So, what are you winding yourself up about in life today? What could you let go of right now that would enable you to connect more with your children?

In this next section, you'll find a range of exercises that will help you to gain a little more control over your feelings – some are designed to calm and soothe and others to uplift and boost your confidence. It's common for us to think about heading to the gym to give our bodies a good work-out but all too often we can forget to exercise the 'muscles of our mind' – that's a pity because with the right kind of exercise, it's possible to get our minds working in a way that serves us better. Which of these activities you choose to do and how often you do them, is up to you. The aim is to help you de-stress and de-clutter your mind so the words and language that you start using with your children can be a little more thought through, rather than off the cuff.

Breathing Exercises

As with anything practice does make perfect, so even if these exercises feel a little strange to begin with, I really do recommend sticking with them:

BASIC BREATHING

1. With your hand on the area above your navel, tighten up your stomach muscles so that they tuck in. Hold the tension for a moment.

2. Now let the muscles relax and feel the difference.

3. Repeat steps 1 and 2. You are now beginning to become aware of what the difference between tension and relaxation in that area feels like.

4. Now breathe in through the nose in such a way that your hand is pushed up by the inflated stomach region. Hold your breath for a moment.

5. Now breathe out through the mouth and notice how your stomach deflates and how this makes your hand go down again.

6. Repeat steps 4 and 5 twenty times and notice how you become progressively calmer as you are doing this exercise.

COUNTING BREATHS

1. Close your eyes.

2. Breathe in so your stomach area rises up, then breathe out and,

in your mind, count '1'. Keep your attention on your breathing only, don't let other thoughts intrude.

3. Continue breathing in and out, and each time you breathe out, count the next number in your mind. Concentrate on your breathing only.

What number did you get to before you found your mind wandering off? To make it easier to get into the higher figures there are a couple of things you can do to help:

a) When you say a number in your mind, create a picture of it too.

b) Focus intently on the various sensations and movements that happen in the trunk of your body while you are breathing in and out.

As your body relaxes, your mind will also begin to feel restful.

MINDFULNESS MADE EASY

We often hear that 'Living in the moment', or 'Mindfulness' can reduce stress and greatly enhance the quality of our lives. Putting it into practice though, can be a lot harder than it sounds – there's nothing more infuriating than having someone tell you to 'just stay calm' when you're feeling anything but. Follow my tips to make this easier.

Based on Buddhist philosophy, 'mindfulness' is a deliberate way of being and research shows that people who practise the art of observation – by deliberately making a point of noticing all the tiny details of each moment – report decreased stress levels, a greater sense of happiness and are less likely to become ill. The benefits are certainly worth having and with just a little bit of practice you too can begin to live your life mindfully.

As our lives become busier and busier, we tend to lose the knack of 'living in the moment' – it's not uncommon for our minds to flip between the past (to things that happened even five minutes ago) and the future (to things that you're planning). It's possible to completely 'miss the moment' in life and stumble through it without ever getting to appreciate the good parts.

How many of us rush through Christmas, for example, with only January's credit card bill as a reminder? Or get so heated up about our children's birthday parties, that we forget to enjoy and savour the moment they blow out the candles on the cake?

TIP NO. 1: Aim to take a few moments each day to keep yourself in the present moment – notice what is going on around you and actively 'create memories' for yourself. Pretend you have a camera in your mind and take imaginary snapshots, noticing the good things as they happen – the smile on someone's face, good food, a sunny day, a feeling of wellbeing. And as you notice each of these events, allow a feeling of gratitude to fill your body

TIP NO. 2: Next time you go for a walk outside, describe everything that you see on your way, quietly to yourself: "I can see a brown dog running past; that lorry has big black wheels; the sun is shining brightly today; I can feel a warm breeze on my face; I can hear the sound of gravel as my feet stride across the path."

You can also practise this on simple activities that you do around the house, such as washing your hands. "I'm turning on the hot tap and now adding some cold water; the soap is green and cold to the touch; I'm squirting some on my left hand and now rubbing it against my right hand; it feels slippery; I am making rich white lather; now I hear the water gurgling down the plughole."

To begin with this may feel rather strange, but remember, being able to associate more fully in your everyday life will heighten your experience of it. Incorporate these tips into your routine every day for a week and notice how your ability to see the fine details rapidly improves. Slowing your mind down in this way will bring a greater sense of peace and happiness into your life.

CREATING A PAUSE BUTTON

Wouldn't life be so much easier if we could simply press a pause button BEFORE we completely lose it, BEFORE we've made those ridiculous threats that we have no intention of keeping and BEFORE we end up saying something so horrible that it hurts us more than it hurts the other person?

Strange as it may seem, it's possible to do just that. Imagination is a very powerful tool and as we know, our bodies will respond to what we're seeing in our mind. So, take a few moments now to create your very own Pause Button.

1. Relax, close your eyes if you need to, and answer these questions.

2. What shape is your pause button and how big is it?

3. What colour is it?

4. Does it have any moving parts?

5. What do you have to do to get life to stop for a moment? Is there a button, a lever or a dial?

6. Whereabouts are you 'seeing' it? Right in front of you or to the side? Up high or low down?

7. Trigger off your pause button right now – do whatever it is that you need to do to it, to get it to work. And at the same time, breathe out slowly – a long, slow breath out.

I don't know exactly what your pause button is going to look like, but I do know that the longer you keep looking at it, the clearer it will become in your mind.

Do this exercise several times today and commit to using this 'pause button' on a regular basis. Each time you feel yourself hitting boiling point, simply conjure up this image and activate your button! Not only will you avoid those unwanted arguments but you'll also reduce the stress and strain you've been placing on your body.

BOOST YOUR CONFIDENCE

We're quick to praise children when they do well – and perhaps even quicker to point out when they don't do so well. Their teachers will write reports and hold progress meetings – it seems to be the natural thing to do if you want your children to grow and develop successfully.

And once we hit the world of work, our lives can seem an endless round of job descriptions, appraisals and meetings with managers and mentors. Pay rises and bonuses let us know that we're on track.

Yet, as soon as we become parents, this structure seems to fall away. Sure, we can see that our children are well and healthy, but as far as our parenting skills go there's no-one to tell us we're doing a good job, point us in the right direction or help us when we struggle. It becomes a trial and error kind of process with most of us listening in on conversations at the school gate hoping to figure out what we should be doing next. No wonder so many of us feel that the confidence we had in our lives before children, has simply been eroded away.

Whether you're hoping to stop those sibling fights, supermarket tantrums, the fussy eating dramas or simply get your children to do their homework and get into bed on time, it will all be so much easier with a large helping of confidence.

"I wish my child had more confidence" is probably the most common request I hear from parents and yet sometimes, we can fail to notice that our own confidence levels are taking a bit of a battering.

Here's a well-known successful NLP visualisation technique that I recommend you work through to change your brain chemistry. It's similar to the 'Circle of Confidence' exercise I showed you in an earlier chapter – only you can do yours sitting down rather than hopping into a circle.

Practising it daily for one week will enable you to give off an aura of someone who feels confident and sure of themselves. Your children will pick up on this altered state and respect you more for it.

Your Confidence Anchor

This simple NLP technique will help you borrow good feelings from past experiences and 'anchor' them to use today. You'll need to read through this exercise and familiarise yourself with it first, as you'll be closing your eyes after the first couple of steps. You could also practice with a friend and have a double boost of confidence – take turns to read out the instructions slowly to each other.

1. Take a few moments to find somewhere comfortable to sit and start by using one of the earlier breathing techniques to start feeling really relaxed.

2. Remind yourself of a time in the past when you felt really confident and good about yourself – it doesn't matter how long ago it was, only that you remember how brilliant you felt. This could be a time at work when you were praised for doing something well, perhaps you'd completed an assignment or project, gave a talk at a conference or managed a small group of people. It could be an achievement on the sports field or a time when you won a competition. It could be a time when you cooked an amazing dinner and received plenty of compliments. It could even be a time when you handled a challenging situation that worried you initially, but you came through

successfully. Remember, no-one is listening to your thoughts right now, so you can just let yourself go and conjure up those images of a time when you felt so, so confident and successful.

3. Close your eyes and take yourself back to that time. See all that you saw, hear all that you heard and feel the feelings that you felt back then. Take your time to do this fully and completely – there's no rush.

4. Become aware of what you're seeing in that picture, and make it a bit bigger. Turn the colours up brighter, bolder, stronger, and if there are any sounds in this memory of yours, turn the volume up louder.

5. Make that picture bigger and bring it closer to you.

6. If you can see yourself in that picture (i.e. you're dissociated), imagine floating up from your chair and sliding down into the 'you' in that picture.

7. Become the YOU and really enjoy this moment once more.

8. This time in the past when you truly felt confident, positive and in control about something.

9. As you continue to enjoy re-living this experience, become aware of where exactly in your body you can feel those feelings of confidence. Are they in your big toe, for example? Or at the end of your nose? Most probably not! So where are they exactly?

10. Locate those feelings and make them spin around even faster, allowing them to spread right through your body from the top of your head to the tips of your toes.

11. Keep running through these steps until you feel that wonderful feeling begin to peak.

12. As it becomes stronger and stronger, just squeeze together the thumb and middle finger on your dominant hand. Squeeze them together tightly, capturing all of those good, good feelings.

13. And release. Relax and open your eyes as you come back into the room. How was that? Good, I hope! And if it wasn't amazing, then I'd like you to pick another example and keep going. You'll soon get the hang of this.

14. Choose 3 different scenarios and run through each one. You'll be strengthening your 'anchor' each time.

15. Whenever you want to feel this confident feeling again, all you're going to have to do is squeeze that thumb and middle finger together once more. You'll have created a powerful association between those confident feelings and the squeezing.

Running through this exercise several times a week will ensure that your 'confident anchor' becomes more powerful. Repetition is the key to getting this right.

You can intensify the feelings attached to this anchor by remembering to squeeze that same thumb and middle finger together whenever you find yourself experiencing other confident moments – or moments that make you just plain feel good, such as laughing at a joke. Do it as it happens.

Once you have established this anchor, you'll be able to summon up those same good feelings automatically, simply by squeezing that thumb and middle finger once more – whenever you need it.

So, next time you want to tackle that dispute over the homework or have a conversation about the time your kids are expected to come home from Saturday night's party, don't do it until you've 'injected' yourself with the feelgood chemicals that this technique will create for you. Nervous parents make children feel nervous and you'll both be releasing those 'flight or fight' hormones that will make any kind of civilized conversation almost impossible.

And don't forget that your internal dialogue – quite literally the conversation you have with yourself inside your head – will also impact on your ability to be successful. Creating a 'doom and gloom' scenario saying things such as *"I don't know why I'm bothering to cook carrots – I bet he doesn't eat them!"* or *"I just know that if I ask him to leave his mobile phone in the hallway, he'll kick off and start shouting at everyone"* isn't going to help you.

Other helpful resources – 'Fix Your Life with NLP'
Relax Now
Boost Your Confidence
Garden of Your Life
CD/MP3s available from www.success-4-kids.com

A Final Note

Now that we've reached the final stages of this programme, I do hope you've enjoyed learning about all the different ways of making parenting children less stressful and more rewarding.

As you've been reading this book, you will have become more open to the idea of making changes and in fact, your subconscious mind is working on new ideas for you all the time now – so remember to notice them and write them down.

Take some time to reflect on the new words and phrases in your 'magic parenting' Dictionary and practice creating sentences of your own – ones that you know will work best in your own situation. Before long, you'll start noticing how easy it is to become a parenting wizard!

In the next section, you'll find your 21-Day Success Journal. I highly recommend that you use this – it's designed to make implementing the strategies easier for you and will help you on your way.

If you'd like to have a separate hard copy – perhaps you're reading this electronically on an e-reader or tablet device or would prefer to fill it in online – then it's possible to download a FREE copy from the Success-4-Kids.com website. Please do take a look. And don't forget that there are many CDs and mp3 downloadable recordings on the website too – all of these are designed to help you.

All that's left for me now is to wish you luck and lots of laughter and happiness in your family life – and I do truly wish that for you. You know, it's all too common for us parents to get frustrated and short-tempered with our children – after all, life is busy and we're in a hurry. Am I right?

But imagine just for a moment that you're rushing to get up a flight of stairs and you encounter an elderly lady in front of you struggling – or perhaps a disabled man on crutches. I suspect most of you would slow down, be patient and offer some help. We would respect that person's limitations and take the delay in our stride, wouldn't we?

Now imagine, that the person on the stairs in front of you is a small child. Too many of us automatically become irritated and it wouldn't be unusual to hear the words *"Can't you hurry up? How many times have I told you to pick those feet up"*.

It's strange, isn't it, how respect for the young person seems to go straight out of the window. And yet, a child is another human being – just like us, only at a different stage of development to ourselves. No more or less valuable than we are.

Whilst my aim in writing this book has been to make the life of parents easier, perhaps it hasn't escaped your notice that my aim has also been to influence a change in the way we speak to our children – for I know the damage that words can do. Words can boost our confidence and fill us with greatness – but words can also harm and hurt.

Now that you have the knowledge, you also have the choice.

It's never too late to 'start all over' and change the relationship that you have with your children – the past is the past, so go forward and live for the future.

Be well, stay happy and keep learning new things!

Alicia

YOUR 21 DAY
SUCCESS JOURNAL

Your 21 Day Success Journal

In this next section, you'll find your 21-Day Success Journal. I highly recommend that you use this – it's designed to make implementing the strategies easier for you and will help you on your way.

Remember, if you would like to have a separate hard copy – perhaps you're reading this electronically on an e-reader or tablet device – or would prefer to be able to fill it in online, then it is possible to download a FREE copy from the Success-4-Kids.com website. Please do take a look.

Too often, it can be easy to quickly notice what's not working well, the times you've tried to implement changes and failed. My aim is to encourage you to do the complete opposite now on a regular basis, so it becomes an automatic habit for you. The more you notice the signs that you're moving in the right direction (and they can be small signs to begin with), the more likely you are to be successful.

If you do not acknowledge, notice and become aware of what works well by gathering proof and evidence, not only are you less likely to get there, but you're more likely to become disheartened, deflated and staying on track and in focus will be so much harder.

After all, no-one likes to feel like a failure; if you don't feel good, you'll stop doing it. If you're attempting to introduce some changes to either routine or behaviour it's going to be important to complete your Journal and regularly ask yourself the question 'what worked well today?'

DAY 1

"If we are facing in the right direction, all we have to do is keep on walking."

BUDDHIST PROVERB

Well done for showing up here – it's good to see you! Now that you're ready for action, use the information you gathered from your Wish List and the goal-setting exercise to write down your targets for today. Aim for at least three and write them here – remember to say what you do want, rather than what you don't want!

-

-

-

DAY 2

"Change starts when someone sees the next step."
WILLIAM DRAYTON

It's good to get into the habit of stepping back and noticing as changes begin to happen.

- What was one positive thing that you noticed about yesterday?

- What are you looking forward to today?

DAY 3

"Your children need your presence more than your presents."

JESSE JACKSON

Organisation, strategies, routines are all good and well but it's good to remember that successful parenting is about so much more than that. Share a special moment with your child today.

• Today's target is:

• What I'm looking forward to tomorrow:

DAY 4

"Learning is not a spectator sport."

D. BLOCHER

How did you spend your special moment with your child yesterday? Did you enjoy it? Did they enjoy it? Did you feel closer as a result?

I'm hoping the answers to those questions are a resounding 'YES'. If they are, then make a note of what it was that you did right – for things that work well, are worth repeating.

And if it didn't work well, then make a note of that too – for you'll want to be sure to avoid doing it next time!

• What I learnt from yesterday's experience:

• Words that work:

• Words that don't work:

DAY 5

"Follow your instincts. That's where true wisdom manifests itself."
OPRAH WINFREY

An aeroplane doesn't reach its' destination by flying in a straight line and neither will you. You may find yourself having to change and alter your course after setting your goals – and that's OK. You'll be receiving new information from your children each and every day, so it's only right that you correct your flight path should you need to.

- Today's target is:

- I've noticed this has been working well:

DAY 6

Keeping that picture in your mind of the bright, shiny, happy future you'll be having with your children, is a sure-fire way of ensuring that you get it – for as you know "what we see is what we get". Take 10 minutes for yourself today, to sit, dream and imagine – no need to feel guilty, for you'll actually be working very hard indeed!

• This is what I saw in my 'dream':

• When I've achieved my dream, it will enable me to:

DAY 7

> *"Before I got married I had six theories about bringing up children;*
> *now I have six children, and no theories..."*
>
> JOHN WILMOT

Congratulations! You've made it through your first week – well done for coming this far. It's a good time to do a review of the words and language patterns that you've started to use.

- New words and language patterns that I've learnt and used well:

- Unhelpful words that I've stopped using, now that I have this new knowledge:

- Words I'm keen to use but haven't tested out yet:

DAY 8

"All great things have small beginnings"

PETER SENGE

Today is a good day to remember the 80/20 Rule. A few small changes will make a big difference to your life and the life of your family.

- Today's target is:

- One positive thing I noticed today:

- What I'm looking forward to tomorrow:

DAY 9

> *"Failure is simply the opportunity to begin again,*
> *this time more intelligently."*
>
> HENRY FORD

Is there something that you're struggling with? 'Modelling' is a great NLP skill that successful people in the world use on a regular basis – all you have to do is COPY someone else. So many times we tell our children off for copying, but actually it's a great way to learn. Is there another parent who just seems to get their kids to do what you'd like yours to do? Then watch closely, observe and listen in to the language patterns being used. Figure out what it is they're doing and pick up some valuable tips.

- Today's target is:

- Tips I picked up today:

DAY 10

> *"If you don't know where you are going, you may end up somewhere else."*
>
> YOGI BERRA

Time for a bit of laughter, methinks. Psychologists and experts say that laughter is one of the best forms of medicine and they're not wrong. Laughter can boost the immune system and give you a feeling of more energy. Think of three ways you could introduce a bit of extra laughter into your day today:

1.

2.

3.

- My children made me laugh today because:

DAY 11

Well, here you are – halfway through your programme. You see, it's going to be easier than perhaps you had originally thought. The reason for choosing 21 Days is because it's a decent chunk of time that's long enough to get those new habits to stick and for the old ones to be broken.

Let's think about habits:

- New habits I've now adopted:

- Old habits I no longer do:

- Words that work:

- Words that don't work:

DAY 12

"If you just keep moving, sooner or later the finish line will show up."
STU MITTLEMAN

What's the difference between a winner and a loser? The winner never gives up. I know that answer seems a little simplistic, but it's true! Taking one small step each day, in the direction of your goal is what is going to ensure that you reach your destination.

Stop and think for a moment today. Is there anything that you tried to do and then quickly gave up because it started to feel difficult? Today is the day to pick it back up again and have another go. The results may be completely different second time around – and if they are, then make sure you notice if there was anything slightly different this time around. That is the difference that made all the difference.

- Three things I am grateful for today:

1.

2.

3.

- Words that work:

DAY 13

"Twenty years from now you will be more disappointed by the things that you didn't do than by the ones that you did do."

MARK TWAIN

So far this Success Journal has focused very much on you – but what about your children? How are they getting on with some of the changes that you've been implementing? Could they do with a little extra help and guidance from you?

Think of one way to spend extra time with each of your children, help them to learn new things and remind them that you love them.

- Today's target is:

- New words I will test out today are:

DAY 14

"Celebrate what you want to see more of."

TOM PETERS

You're two weeks into the programme – well done! It's time for a treat – how will you let yourself know that you've worked hard and you're pleased with yourself? It's important to take some time out just for you – for the better you feel, the better able you will be to take care of all the important people in your life.

Today I will do three things for myself:

1.

2.

3.

DAY 15

Today, it's time to share a secret with a friend. Think of one person who you could tell about the programme that you've been following – the changes that you've made and the results you've had. It only needs to be one small change and one small success – telling someone else makes it concrete and real, rather than just an abstract idea in your mind. The more real it is, the more likely it is to stick.

- Today I noticed this worked well:

- Today I noticed that this wasn't working so well:

- I shared this secret:

DAY 16

"You make mistakes – mistakes do not make YOU."

MAXWELL MALTZ

You've come a long way – that's 16 days of new behaviours that will become new habits that could stick for the rest of your life. So, let's make sure they're really good ones. Yesterday, you were noticing what wasn't working so well – what are you going to do about it? Are you going to change your approach or drop the idea completely? It's fine to be honest and admit when something you thought you wanted, you in fact, no longer do. But if it's something that would truly make your life better, easier and happier, then don't get stuck, get clever. Ask an expert, speak to a friend, read a book, look online, visit the library – someone already has the solution to your particular problem. Find them and you'll be making progress.

- My goal today is:

- This helped me today

- Words that work:

DAY 17

"People often say that motivation doesn't last. Well, neither does bathing – that's why we recommend it daily."

ZIG ZIGLAR

It's time for a walk in the fresh air. Practice your Mindfulness skills by slowly walking in nature for 10 minutes. Describe everything that you see, feel, hear and smell as you do. Finish up by taking a photo on your mobile phone of something that touched or pleased you.

- Today's target is:

- The improvements that I've noticed so far are:

- My children made me laugh today because:

DAY 18

*"However beautiful the strategy, you should occasionally
look at the results."*

WINSTON CHURCHILL

How are your Family Meetings going? I hope you have been able
to have a few by now and are finding them useful. Next time you're
having a brainstorming session, you could introduce the wearing
of hats – this may sound unusual but it's based on an idea
developed by creative thinker Edward de Bono. Each hat represents
a different perspective and you can all take turns to wear each one.
For example: the white hat wearer could present the facts or topic
to be discussed; the blue hat will give details of the process – how
the idea will be carried out; the green hat will be responsible for
putting forward creative ideas; the yellow hat will put forward the
positive outlook – and the black hat will play devil's advocate,
saying what they feel could go wrong. You can play around with
this idea and change it to suit yourselves.

- Our next Family Meeting will be:

- Ideas to discuss at the next Meeting:

- Words that work:

DAY 19

"There's no such thing as bad weather – only the wrong clothes"

BILLY CONNOLLY

How are you getting on with re-framing your children's complaints and objections? Have you noticed how putting a positive spin on everything changes the mood of the house? You can practice this by creating a game that the whole family can play. Each person has to come up with a truly negative statement and the rest of the family members can take turns to put a positive spin on it. For example: *"I lost my pencil case today; I ate too much chocolate and felt sick afterwards; the dog ran into the house with his muddy paws…"*. You can be creative and come up with some pretty ridiculous statements too – ones that will make everyone laugh. The content of this game doesn't really matter, for the aim is to encourage the mind to think in a more positive way and learn how to be creative.

- Today I will use this new word:

- What I'm looking forward to tomorrow:

- Words that work:

DAY 20

"Home is where one starts from"

T.S. ELIOT

We're nearly at the end of the programme now, so I hope you've been making progress. Most of the time, I've been encouraging you to look at very small details – changing or moving your words around. But now, I'd like to remind you to also look at the big picture – your home, your overall environment. It's not uncommon to find parents who will bend over backwards for their guests and treat them with respect – only to expect their children to struggle and adjust to the surroundings. What changes could you make around the home, to make your child's life easier? A child-height mirror, hook or table, perhaps? Labels on storage boxes or photos to use as points of reference.

- Changes I am thinking of making:

1.

2.

3.

- Words that work:

DAY 21

> *"If you want happiness for an hour – take a nap.*
> *If you want happiness for a day – go fishing.*
> *If you want happiness for a year – inherit a fortune.*
> *If you want happiness for a lifetime – help someone else."*
>
> CHINESE PROVERB

CONGRATULATIONS! I am delighted that you have come so far. After 21 Days of thinking about words and new language patterns, I know that you will have made some positive changes and your children will have benefited too.

The words and phrases that I've described in this book are not magic – but they might seem like magic. Over time and sooner than you would imagine, these strategies will transform your daily life. But, you probably already know that, don't you?

- What I'm most proud of myself for:

- What I'm most proud of my children for:

- Our family treat is going to be:

Index

absorb 14
adapt 14
adrenaline rush 85, 87, 107
alternative 34
anchor, anchoring 75,110
anxiety 84, 88, 96
attitude 29
auditory 46, 130, 132

Bannister, Roger 113
bedtime routine 176
bedwetting 86, 116, 121
beliefs 113, 199
blushing 107
brain chemistry 106
brainwash 11
breathing techniques 87
but reversal 31

cause and effect 41
central nervous system 24
change 29, 33
childhood imprinting 15
choice, illusion of 37
Circle of Confidence 114, 109
clinical hypnotherapist 18
closed questions 42
comfort zone 102
command 34
commitment 26
complaints 44
confidence 50, 101, 109
Confidence Anchor 112, 114
conflict 31
conscious eating 166
conscious mind 12, 13
critical voice 20

dejection 30
descriptive praise 51
desire 31
Disaster Movie 121

Eighty / Twenty rule 214
embarrassment 107
emotional hunger 167
emotional make-up 15
endorphins 87
Enuresis Clinic 122
exams 138
exhibitionist 16, 17

family values 77, 102, 199
fear 84, 93, 94
feedback sandwich 212
fight or flight response 60, 85, 107, 241
framework for objections 37
fussy-eating 146

generalised anxiety 86
give a reason 40
goals 219

habits 116
hair-pulling 116, 159
hypnosis 9, 10, 15
hypnotic mind 12
hypnotic state 18
hypnotise 10, 11
hypnotist 17, 18

identity 102
illusion of choice 37
images 26

imagination 20, 26
implied causative 35
influence 19
internal dialogue 20, 108, 183, 229, 241

junk food cravings 159

kinaesthetic 46, 130, 131

language of persuasion 11
language patterns 6, 19, 39, 55
leading questions 45
learning preferences 129
lost performative 42, 43

Magic TV Control 94
Magic Stop Button 66
magnetically 20, 22, 25
matching, pacing, leading 62
melatonin 177
mind reading 47
mindfulness 96, 234
mood swings 86
motivation 31, 32, 49
moving forward 45

nail-biting 38, 116
negative pictures 24, 26, 27
night terrors 86
negative thinking 105
negative words 22, 23, 24, 28
Now I Can See exercise 182

objections 32
obstacles 25
open questions 42
overcoming problems 45

Pause Button 236
persuade 19
phobia 85
positive 23, 28
positive pictures 26
positive thinking 106
possibility 29
praise 48, 51, 208
preferences 46
presuppositions 36, 43
programming 14, 16
progression 33

questions, open and closed 42

rapport 43
reason, give a 40
reflective listening 44
rejection 30
relaxation 89
resilience 102, 103, 104
resistance 34
reversal 31
reverse psychology 120, 127
rewards 119, 142

screen time 76
self-care 225
self-esteem 43, 48, 54, 102
self-fulfilling prophecy 12, 71, 75
self-image 52, 72, 231
selfie culture 102
serotonin 106
sibling rivalry 65, 200
sleep – Gradual Withdrawal 178
sleep – Immediate Withdrawal 180
sleeplessness 86
Spelling Cure 136
stage hypnosis 9, 10, 15
stage performance 16, 17
stage show 18
stammers 86
stress 85, 144
subconscious mind 10, 12, 13, 14, 93, 116, 117
substitution 119
success plan 221
suggestibility tests 16
supermarket tantrums 73

thoughts 24
thumb-sucking 86, 116, 118
tics 86, 116
trance 18
transformation 33
transient 29

visualisation process 23
visualise 23, 34
visual 46, 68, 130
visualisation exercises 124, 143

weight loss 165
Words that Don't Work 52-55

Words that Work:
-always 28
-and 30
-become 33
-but 30, 31, 32
-but reversal 31
-can't 29
-could 25
-don't 22
-it's 42
-let's 42
-like you 43
-listen 35
-may 25
-might 25
-must 25
-never 28
-no 22
-not 22
-ought to 25
-should 25
-sometimes 28
-stop 34
-tell you 34
-that is 42
-think about it 35
-try 27
-when 35
worries and worrying 91, 92
Worry Box 92

Yes Set 39
Yes Weekend 38

ABOUT THE AUTHOR

Originally a *Montessori Teacher*, Alicia ran her own School for five years and followed this up with further training and studies at the Anna Freud Centre in London. She then went on to train as an *Integrative Psychotherapist & Clinical Hypnotherapist* in 2003, as well as undertaking numerous trainings in *NLP (Neuro-Linguistic Programming)* with Paul McKenna and Richard Bandler, assisting with their seminars for many years. She's now a qualified *Trainer of NLP* running workshops on a variety of topics, including parenting.

She's run a successful practice, for both adults and children, in London's Harley Street since 2004. Her unique blend of psychology and practical parenting advice means she's the number one choice for parents when it comes to fixing children's bad habits and behaviours.

She's the author of best-selling books: *'Stop Bedwetting in 7 Days'* (MX Publishing, 2009; 2nd edition Matador, 2012) and *'Fix Your Life with NLP'* (Simon & Schuster, 2012). Her work is regularly featured in the media.

She lives in Hertfordshire and is mum to three grown-up children. Visit websites for more information:

www.aliciaeaton.co.uk
www.success-4-kids.com
www.stopbedwettingin7days.co.uk

USEFUL CONTACT DETAILS:

GENERAL HYPNOTHERAPY STANDARDS COUNCIL
The General Hypnotherapy Standards Council (GHSC) and General Hypnotherapy Register (GHR) are the UK's largest and most prominent organisations within the field of Hypnotherapy and together present an exemplary model for the simultaneous protection of the public and the provision of practitioner credibility and services. You can find a register of practising hypnotherapists at: www.general-hypnotherapy-register.com

CONTEMPORARY COLLEGE OF THERAPEUTIC STUDIES
Provides validated integrated psychotherapy, practical hypnotherapy and counselling training courses in London.
www.contemporarycollege.com

NLP LIFE TRAINING
Provides a range of training courses and seminars in Neuro-Linguistic Programming for use in therapeutic, personal, coaching and corporate contexts.
www.nlplifetraining.com

THE MARIA MONTESSORI INSTITUTE
Provides authentic AMI Montessori teacher training, schools and reaches out to underprivileged communities.
www.mariamontessori.org

MONTESSORI SOCIETY AMI
The Montessori Society is affiliated to the Association Montessori Internationale (AMI). It aims to inform teachers and parents about Montessori and its practice. It runs seminars and workshops and sells Montessori books.
www.montessorisociety.org.uk